the s

chamonix

mont-blanc

first edition 2003

written and edited by
Michael Kayson & Isobel Rostron

winter press
www.snowmole.com

the snowmole guide to **chamonix mont-blanc**
first edition 2003

published by winter press
45 Mysore Road London SW11 5RY

printed by Cambrian Printers
Llanbadarn Road Aberystwyth Ceredigion SY23 3TN

ISBN 0-9545739-1-9

A catalogue record of this book is available from the British Library.

snowmole does not accept any advertising or payment, and the guides are written completely free from any bias.

contents

about snowmole

snowmole / snṓmōl / n. & v. **1** a spy operating within alpine territory (esp. ski resorts) for the purpose of gathering local knowledge. **2** (in full **snowmole guide**) the guidebook containing information so gathered. v. research or compile or process intelligence on an alpine resort or surrounding mountainous area.

the idea

How much you enjoy your winter holiday depends on a variety of things. Some you cannot influence - you can't guarantee sunshine, good snow, or your flight landing on time... but most things should be within your control. With the majority of ski holidays lasting just a week or less, you don't want to waste time trying to find a good restaurant, or struggling with an overgrown piste map. The snowmole guides are designed with two purposes in mind: to save you time by providing essential information on the operation of the resort, and to help you to make the most of your time by giving insight into every aspect of your stay.

how to use the guide

The guide is not intended to be read from cover to cover. It is split into four distinct sections, and some information will be useful to you beforehand, some while you are in resort, some while on the mountain.

getting started deals with the basics: how to get to the resort, how to get around once you're there, and your options when buying your lift pass, renting equipment and booking lessons or mountain guides.

the skiing gives an overview of the mountains and the ski areas, contains detailed descriptions of pistes and lifts as well as a section covering the off-piste, and a breakdown for beginners, intermediates, experts, boarders and non-skiers.

the resort covers the best of the rest of your holiday: a series of reviews on where to eat, where to play, where to stay and what to do when skiing isn't an option. Some reviews are extended as 'features', and everything is cross-referenced to either the valley or the town map.

the a-z comprises a directory of contact details and information, from accidents to weather, a glossary of terms used in this guide and in skiing in general, and an index to help navigate your way around the guide.

maps

The guide features maps designed and produced specifically for snowmole. While the information they contain is as accurate as possible, some omissions have been made for the sake of clarity. An explanation of the town and valley maps can be found on page 15 and of the piste maps on the inside back cover.

Once you know where you want to go, you need to decide how you want to get there. Traditionally, most skiing holidays are booked though travel agents or tour operators, but with the advent of cheap flights, DIY holidays are becoming more popular. There are pros and cons to both.

DIY v package

package

The theory behind package holidays is that all you should have to think about is getting from the top of the slopes to the bottom. The core of every package deal is convenience - though it comes wrapped in all kinds of paper. Ski companies fall into two distinct categories: large mainstream operators, and smaller more specialist ones. The mainstream brand offers ready-made holidays, where everything is already planned and you take it or leave it. Trips with smaller companies can be more expensive, but tend to be more flexible and many tailor the trip to your exact requirements. Alternatively, if you don't want to be restricted to one operator, a travel agent will have access to a selection of holidays offered by several companies.

flights - mainstream companies only run week-long trips, from Saturday to Saturday or Sunday to Sunday - giving you 6 days on the slopes and 7 nights in (or on) the town. They charter their own flights - making the holiday cheaper - but you have little option as to when or from where you travel. Smaller ski companies give you greater choice - many specialise in long weekends for the 'money-rich, time-poor' market, with departures on Thursday evenings and returns on Monday evenings, giving you 4 days skiing for 2 days off work... but the real advantage is their use of scheduled flights, so you can pick the airport, airline, and when you travel.

transfers - with a mainstream company, your journey to resort will be by coach, with others who have booked through the same company. You may have to wait for other flights, and on the way there may be stop-offs in other resorts or at other accommodation before your own. Because you're travelling at the weekend the journey tends to take longer. With a smaller company you may transfer by coach, minibus, taxi, or car depending on how much you've paid and the size of your group. And if you arrive mid-week, the transfers tend to be quicker.

accommodation - where you stay depends entirely on who you book with. Different companies have deals with different hotels, some specialise in chalets, some operate in specific resorts... the limiting factor is what's in the brochure - though if you want to stay in a particular hotel, a more specialist company may try to organise it for you.

in resort - some companies offer a drop-off and pick-up service from the lifts, which is a huge benefit in sprawling resorts. But the main benefit of a package holiday is the resort rep. From the moment you arrive to the moment you leave, there is someone whose job it is to ensure your holiday goes smoothly... or that's the theory. More than likely your rep will sort out lift passes and equipment rental. Some will organise evening activities and be available for a short period every day to answer questions. Most are supported by an in situ manager who deals with more serious issues. The more you pay for your holiday, the better your rep should be. The best are service-oriented French speakers... but it is difficult to recruit hard-working, intelligent, bilingual people to work for next to nothing. If you want to know what - or who - to expect, ask when you book.

DIY

If you DIY, you have more control over the kind of holiday you take and what you pay. But as you have to make all the arrangements, you'll need more time to plan the trip.

flights - BA, bmibaby, Swiss, and Easyjet schedule regular flights to Geneva (the best international aiport for Chamonix). You can fly from all major UK airports, though the cheapest flights are normally from London, and the earlier you book the cheaper it will be. The airlines accept reservations for the upcoming winter from around June or July. Some chartered airlines such as Monarch or Thomas Cook airlines may also have a limited number of seats for sale.

If you don't want to fly, the excellent European motorway system makes driving to the Alps surprisingly easy. Getting there by train is also an option, though there may be some distance between your arrival station and your resort.

transfers - from Geneva, you can get to your resort by road and to some by train - see **travel to chamonix**.

accommodation - on a DIY trip you are not restricted by brochures or company deals... however the easiest way to book a chalet or an apartment is through a company or website offering accommodation only, such as Interhome or ifyouski.com. You can liaise with the owners directly if you can find their details, but this is often difficult. For hotels you might be able to get a discount off the published price by contacting them directly.

in resort - this is perhaps where the difference between DIY and package is most noticeable. There is no rep on hand so you have to buy your own lift pass, organise your own equipment rental... but this can have its pluses: you can be sure that you get exactly the right type of pass and you can choose which rental shop you use.

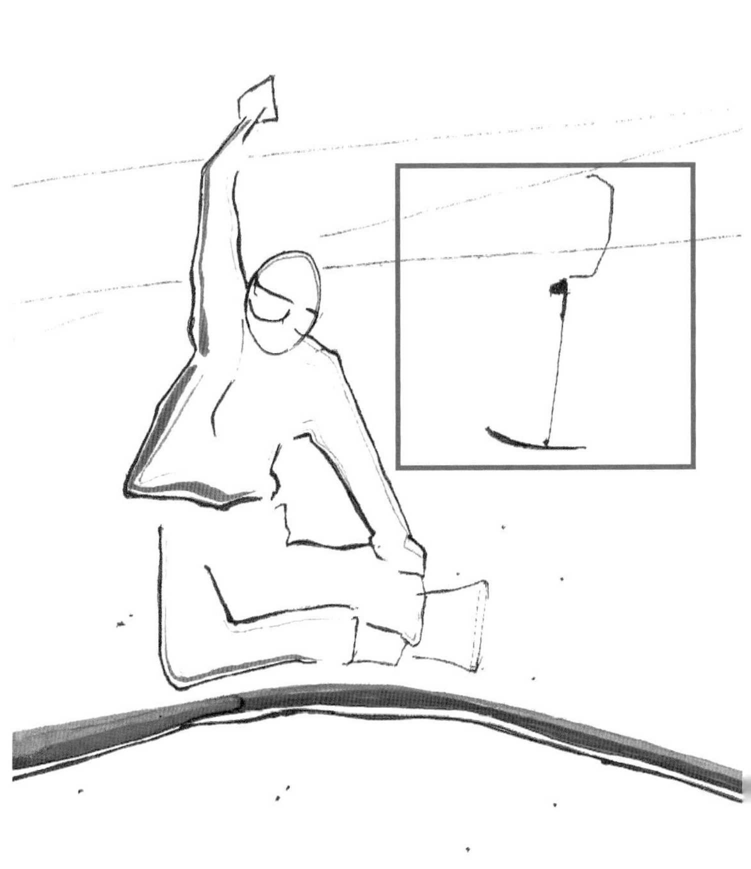

getting started

chamonix mont-blanc

Almost everything about Chamonix is different from a typical ski resort. It is renowned for being the extreme skiing capital of the world - and indeed much of the steepest, narrowest and most dangerous skiing in the Alps can be found in the valley - but there is far more to Chamonix than that. While the surrounding mountains make it a mecca for climbers and mountaineers as well as skiers and snowboarders, there is plenty of on- and off-snow activity for those less inclined to danger. Perhaps the truest thing that can be said is that people do not go there to be seen - they go there to have been. Chamonix has few pretensions, and the fashion is more for Dakine backpacks than for Prada ski outfits. While it is expensive it does not even approach Val d'Isère or Courchevel prices, and while you can stay in a luxury 4* hotel you can also stay in a €12/night dormitory. There are some excellent restaurants and the most diverse après in the Alps, but people go there to ski.

snapshot

highs...
- some of the best skiing in the Alps
- the Vallée Blanche
- large and diverse town
- 1 hour from Geneva airport
- can be done cheaply

and lows
- ski areas not linked
- limited gentle skiing
- high on-piste speed
- very busy town with lots of traffic
- logistically difficult for mixed ability groups

That said, it is not for everyone. The skiing is not gentle, the view from the town is as intimidating as it is spectacular, there is no ski-in/ski-out accommodation, the valley's ski areas are separate and the only way between them is by road... but Chamonix has a charm quite unlike anywhere else. Whether you are drinking coffee by the river, practising turns on the pistes, or skiing the Vallée Blanche, there is something compelling about being under the gaze of Mont Blanc. And people either like it or they don't.

the resort

Chamonix is much larger than a typical resort, and is a fully functional town in its own right. It is effectively divided into two: the centre of town - a bustling blend of bars, restaurants, shops and hotels; and Chamonix Sud, which has its own distinct flavour but which is predominantly made up of mid-grade hotels and apartment blocks.

The town is not really an attractive place, and with its popularity increasing every year the little old world charm that remains is being tightly squeezed by commercial progress. In contrast, the narrow valley down which the Arve river flows is surprisingly spacious and outstandingly beautiful. Only Chamonix and Argentière are well developed, and very little of the mountain area is tainted by lifts and pistes.

who goes there

In short, everyone. In high season the tourist population is over a third English - so if you're looking for an authentic French getaway, Chamonix is the wrong place to find it. Along with the English, it is most popular with Swedes and other Scandinavians, though its worldwide renown also draws Russians, Americans, and a surprising number of non-skiing Asian tourists. It is a popular weekend destination for the French, and with its proximity to two borders a lot of day-trippers come over from Italy and Switzerland.

après

Thanks to the size of the town, there is enough diversity in the after-ski department to cater for every price range and pretty much every taste. The always-busy après scene is traditionally centred on the Rue des Moulins, a cobbled pedestrian street which offers five bars, four restaurants, two cafés and a night club - but the rest of the town has an almost limitless choice of crowded sports bars, welcoming local pubs, riverside cafés, or whatever takes your fancy. You won't be bored.

the skiing

Chamonix's best - and worst - aspect is its skiing. Its reputation for steep, unforgiving runs is well deserved, and there is enough on-piste challenge to provide a workout for even the most advanced skiers. There is also plenty of intermediate level skiing, enormous off-piste opportunity and ample provision for beginners.

By name the four areas are the Brévent, the Flégère, the Grands Montets, and Le Tour. Only the Brévent and the Flégère are linked, so if you are staying in Chamonix the only way to the Grands Montets and Le Tour is by road. This is the root of most of the complaints about the skiing - to catch the first lift at Le Tour you can't just roll out of bed at 8:30am and crawl to the gondola station, because it's about 10km away.

temperatures

It's fairly easy to generalise temperatures - December and January are usually the coldest months, with things warming up gradually through February, March and April. When you are in resort, don't be fooled by appearances - it will often be colder when there is a cloudless, blue sky than when snow is falling. Temperatures can range from -15°C at ground level on the coldest days to as high as 20°C later on in the season when the sun is shining.

snowfall

When and how much snow falls varies from year to year, but general trends do emerge. Snow falls sporadically on the upper slopes throughout the year. Snow cannons along the line of the Bochard lift make the Grands Montets the first area to open, usually in late November. By Christmas, there is usually enough snow cover to open everything except the runs down to Chamonix and Les Praz. The snow normally continues to fall through January and historically snow levels peak in February, in time for the busiest weeks. As temperatures rise in March, the snow levels drop again. Late season snow is common, though the falls are less sustained and because of the higher temperatures, what falls doesn't last as long on the upper slopes, and lower down barely settles at all.

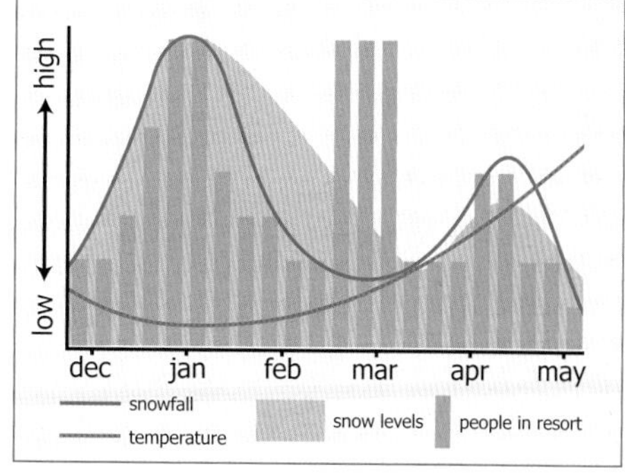

volume of people in resort

As Chamonix has the largest seasonnaire population in the Alps, the town is never quiet - though the slopes are still significantly less busy in low season. Like most other major resorts, it is busy over Christmas and New Year, and very busy for two weeks in February during the English and French school half-terms. Uniquely, Chamonix's busiest week is in early March - the week of the ChamJam, a world famous series of boarding and skiing events on the Grand Montets. Check before you book for the actual date - and if you aren't going specifically to see the ChamJam, don't go when it's on.

getting there

One of Chamonix's many attractions is how easy it is to reach: you can wake up in London and be on the slopes of the Brévent by lunchtime. Below are details of the various ways of getting yourself to the mountains.

All contact details for the transport listed can be found in the **directory**.

by air to geneva

You can fly to Geneva from any major airport in England - see **planning your trip**.

the airport - Geneva airport is small and easy to navigate. On your right as you come through the gate into the arrivals hall there is a small café, followed by the lost luggage counter and a small restaurant. There are toilets in both directions. The car park and the taxi rank are straight out of the door, and France is off to the right about 10km away. If you want a decent meal and it is daytime, then head up the escalator to departures and up again to the shopping area. There is a good quality boulangerie next to the bar at the far right-hand end of the terminal.

Once you have safely landed in Geneva, you can get to Chamonix in one of five ways.

by hire car - you can hire a car at Geneva airport by booking over the phone, on the internet, or when you arrive at the airport. Your car will have the necessary equipment required to legally travel on French roads such as an emergency triangle but you will need to specifically request snow chains and a roof box if you want them.

The journey from Geneva is less than 60 miles (around 90km) and is two-lane motorway all the way. It takes about an hour - though if you are travelling on a Saturday expect traffic and delays. Chamonix Mont-Blanc is clearly signed and you barely need to make a turn, so it is very difficult to go wrong. From the airport follow the green signs to France - you will reach customs within about 15 minutes. Once you are in France, join the A40 heading south-east and follow signs to Chamonix Mont-Blanc, on the Autoroute Blanche (White Motorway). There are two *péage* (toll) stops on the motorway - each will cost around €3. You can pay with cash or by credit card.

by public bus - buses run every day between Geneva airport and the train station in Chamonix. There are four services each way on weekdays and five each way at weekends. The service is much like the National Express, and the journey takes just over 2 hours.

by private bus - ATS (Airport Transfer Service) is basically just a taxi company, but as the name suggests it specialises in transfers, and getting to Chamonix in an ATS minibus is significantly less expensive than in a private taxi.

by train - there is no direct train service between Geneva airport and Chamonix - you have go to Annecy or Annemasse and change, and to get to either of those you have to go to Geneva mainline station and change. If you are competent at finding the right platforms, the journey will take you around 2 hours.

by taxi - taxi is an expensive alternative, but if you are too tired to drive there yourself or have a phobia of public transport, a one-way trip from Geneva airport will cost you approximately €150.

by road

self-drive - the most common starting place for any road journey to the Alps is Calais. You can reach Calais from the UK by the Eurotunnel or ferry. It is then just under 600 miles (a little over 900km) from Calais to Chamonix, and the journey can be done in 10 hours or less. The mustard town of Dijon is about two-thirds of the way if you want to make an overnight stop.

Take the A26 south-east to Reims, then south to Troyes. From there go east on the A5 towards Chaumont then turn south on the A31 to Dijon. From Dijon the A39 takes you south-east and then south past Lons-le-Saunier to Bourg-en-Bresse where you join the A40 south. Stay on the A40 as it bends east and runs past the south tip of Lake Geneva (though you never enter Switzerland) and continues east all the way to Chamonix Mont-Blanc.

There are two *péage* (toll) stops on the route south through France, for which you collect a ticket as you enter the motorway and hand it in as you leave. Between these two and the two stops on the Autoroute Blanche (see previous page) you should expect to pay around €50 in total - you can pay with cash or by credit card.

If the scenery around Lake Geneva tempts you into taking a detour through Switzerland, you will have to buy a *vignette*, a windscreen sticker which acts like a motorway pass (the equivalent of the French *péage*). It costs around €25, and is good for the duration of the year in which you buy it. If you haven't got one before you get there, you can buy one at the border control.

coach - Eurolines run a direct service between London and Chamonix three times a week in each direction. The journey takes about 19 hours and you travel overnight.

calais - chamonix (585miles)

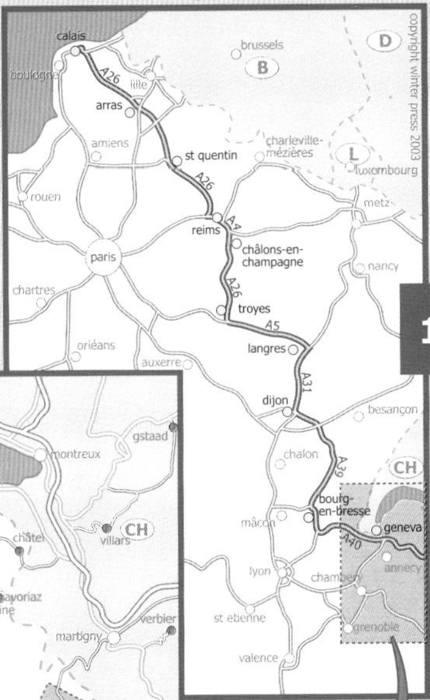
calais
boulogne
brussels
B
D
A26
lille
arras
amiens
st quentin
charleville-mézières
L
luxembourg
rouen
metz
reims
A4
châlons-en-champagne
paris
nancy
chartres
A26
troyes
A5
orléans
langres
auxerre
A31
dijon
besançon
chalon
A39
CH
bourg-en-bresse
mâcon
geneva
A40
annecy
lyon
chambery
st etienne
grenoble
valence
copyright winter press 2003

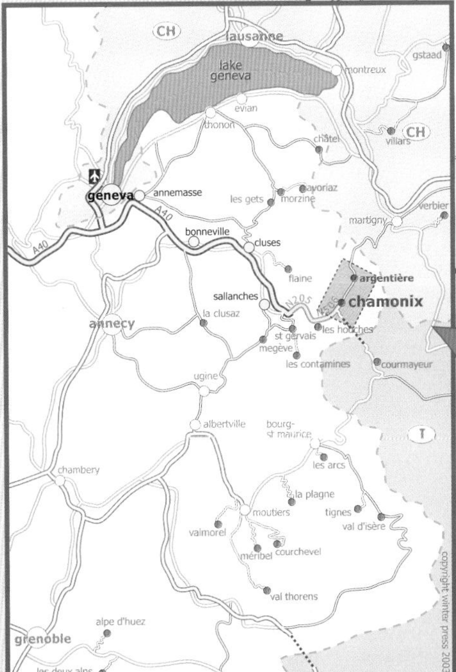
CH
lausanne
lake geneva
montreux
gstaad
evian
thonon
châtel
CH
villars
avoriaz
geneva
annemasse
les gets
morzine
A40
verbier
martigny
A40
bonneville
cluses
flaine
argentière
sallanches
chamonix
N205
annecy
la clusaz
st gervais
les houches
megève
les contamines
courmayeur
ugine
albertville
bourg-st maurice
I
les arcs
chambery
la plagne
moutiers
tignes
val d'isère
valmorel
méribel
courchevel
val thorens
alpe d'huez
grenoble
les deux alps
copyright winter press 2003

geneva - chamonix (57miles)

by train

In theory travelling by train gives you more time in resort - 8 days instead of the usual 6. It's an excellent service if you live in London and are skiing in the 3 Vallées or the Espace Killy, but it doesn't work out so well for a skiing holiday in Chamonix. Unless you travel by TGV, the stops in the Alps are Moutiers and Bourg-St. Maurice. There isn't a direct train service to Chamonix from either of these stations, so the only real way to complete your journey is by car, which will take at least 2 hours.

If you are still undeterred, be sure to book well ahead, as the services become full months in advance.

snowtrain - the Snowtrain is the classic way to travel by train to the Alps. You check in at Dover on Friday afternoon, take a ferry to Calais where you board a *couchette* (a train with sleeping compartments) and travel overnight, arriving in the Alps on Saturday morning. The return service leaves the following Saturday evening.

eurostar overnight - this service leaves London Waterloo on Friday evenings. You travel directly to Paris, where you change onto a *couchette* to travel overnight, arriving in the Alps on Saturday morning. The return service leaves on Saturday evening.

eurostar direct - a daytime service, which leaves London Waterloo on Saturday mornings and arrives in the Alps on Saturday evenings. The return trip departs on Saturday evening.

TGV - if you're intent on travelling by train, the TGV takes you more directly to Chamonix - or at least to Annecy, from where you take a SNCF train on the Saint Gervais/Le Fayet-Vallorcine line, which stops in Chamonix. There is a direct service for Annecy from the Gare de Lyon in Paris. The total journey from Paris to Annecy takes approximately 5 hours. To get to Paris, you can either fly or take the Eurostar.

getting around

using the maps

This guide features a number of maps of the town and valley. They are designed specifically for use with the guide, and as with the ski maps, some omissions and changes have been made for the sake of clarity. Fully comprehensive town maps are available from the tourist office.

valley map - the valley map (on page 17) details the area surrounding Chamonix town, and is contoured in the same way as the ski maps. It shows towns, main connecting roads, bus stops, train lines and ski areas, and highlights the area detailed in the Chamonix and Argentière town maps. It is sectioned by a grid, which is used for reference throughout the guide.

town map - the inside front cover shows the town, highlighting main pedestrian routes and showing main buildings and landmarks, bus stops, car parks, train lines, and road names. The map is sectioned by a grid, which is used for reference throughout the guide.

review maps - at the end of each section of reviews the town map is reproduced in grey, with the places reviewed shown in colour, and named on a key.

minimaps - throughout the review section there are small-scale maps, designed to show the location of 'features', and of places in the reviews that do not appear on the town map. The minimaps either enlarge a small section of the valley map or serve as an extension of the town map, and they show main buildings, bus stops and car parks.

snapshot

from chamonix by road
chamonix valley
argentière 10 mins
les praz 5 mins
le tour 15 mins

other resorts
courmayeur (italy) 20 mins
les houches 10 mins
megève 30 mins
morzine 45 mins
verbier (switzerland) 1 hour

the valley

With no traffic it's about a 15 minute journey from Chamonix to Le Tour - but with a lot of cars on the road it can take upwards of 45 minutes. Unless your hotel or tour operator provides transport, your options are either to take the bus or to drive.

by bus - given the enormous number of people that use the Chamonix Bus every day, it is remarkably efficient. You will rarely have to wait for more than 10 or 15 minutes for a bus to turn up, and at peak times they come more frequently - though of course they are far busier. There are a variety of services, most of which loop around the ski areas, but some of which simply shuttle to Chamonix's satellite towns - so make sure you check the destination on the front of the bus. The service is free with the ChamSki lift pass. Bus stops are marked on the town and valley maps.

There are also night buses between Chamonix and Argentière - one bus runs every hour in each direction between 8pm-11:45pm.

by car - this is by far the easiest way around the valley - no waiting, no queuing, more than a square foot of personal space during the journey... if you have your own transport all you have to worry about is the traffic, which can be considerable at peak times - Chamonix is subject to a rush hour in much the same way as a busy English town. There are plenty of pay car parks in Chamonix, marked on the town map. There is also parking along many of the roads in town, which is pay & display during the day but free over lunchtime (the *gendarmerie* who dish out the tickets are on siesta between 12pm and 2:30pm) and in the evenings.

For specific information on getting to and parking at each ski area, see the relevant entries in **the skiing**.

the town

Chamonix is big for a ski resort, but by no means so big that you need to drive around town - it takes about 20 minutes to walk from one end to the other. The town centre is largely pedestrianised, and while there is some traffic through the middle it is very slow moving. The Brévent and the Aiguille du Midi are within walking range of town, and you can get to the Flégère on the cable car liaison - but the Grands Montets and Le Tour are only accessible by road.

finding your way

Though restaurants, bars, shops and so on are well spread throughout the town, in general the areas are divided as follows: the Place Balmat (**town e3**), Place Sassure (**e3**) and the pedestrian cobbles of the Rue des Moulins (**e3/4**) are home to bars, cafés and restaurants; the main shopping is split between the Avenue Michel Croz (**e3**) and the long stretch from the Rue Joseph Vallot (**f4**) to the end of the Rue du Docteur Paccard (**c4**). The best spot to catch a bus is on the Avenue du Mont Blanc (**f3**) at the end of the Rue des Moulins, and the best place to get off for the town centre is at the end of the Rue Whymper (**e2**). In Chamonix Sud the main drag is the Avenue de l'Aiguille du Midi (**b/c3**), and the main bus stop is next to the Bowling Pub (**a3/4**).

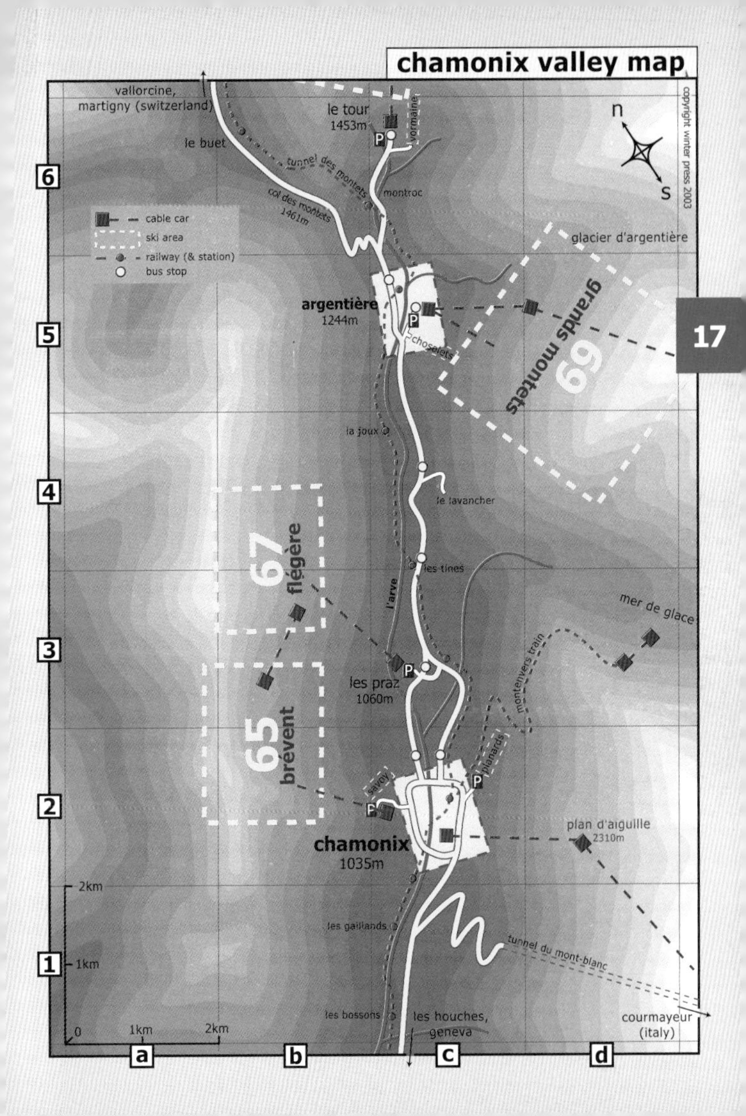
chamonix valley map
copyright winter press 2003
n
s
vallorcine,
martigny (switzerland)
le buet
le tour
1453m
vormaine
tunnel des montets
col des montets
1461m
montroc
cable car
ski area
railway (& station)
bus stop
glacier d'argentière
argentière
1244m
chosalets
grands montets
69
la joux
le lavancher
67
flégère
les tines
l'arve
mer de glace
montenvers train
les praz
1060m
65
brévent
planards
savoy
chamonix
1035m
plan d'aiguille
2310m
2km
1km
0
les gaillands
tunnel du mont-blanc
les bossons
les houches,
geneva
courmayeur
(italy)
6
5
4
3
2
1
a
b
c
d

accommodation

At the end of a day on the slopes, you probably won't mind where you rest your head. But when planning your holiday, you might put a bit more thought into where you stay. For a ski resort, Chamonix has a mind-boggling range of accommodation, with over 70 hotels in addition to countless chalets, apartments, gîtes and dormitories.

useful information

access - none of the Chamonix or Argentière accommodation is ski-in/ski-out. Some places are more convenient for the Aiguille du Midi, some for the Brévent, and Argentière is best for skiing the Grands Montets. But unless you have your own car you will have to use the bus to get around the valley no matter where you stay. Most hotels have a bus stop nearby.

availability - accommodation throughout the valley is available more or less year round - Chamonix thrives in summer as well as winter. Most hotels close for three weeks or a month during May, and some again for the same period in October.

price - there is something for all budgets. Prices rise in the high season and are at their lowest at the beginning and end of the season, when there is also more availability.

chalet, apartment or hotel

chalets

Surprisingly few of the mainstream operators offer chalet holidays in Chamonix. Most are either privately owned or run by smaller and more specialist companies.

tour operator - the chalet package includes bed, breakfast, afternoon tea, and on 6 nights out of 7 an evening meal with wine. You will be looked after by one or more commonly two English chalet hosts. Mainstream operators will also organise your flights and transfers. The more you pay, the better you can expect the quality of everything to be. Some companies offer discounts to big groups and families. Unless you book the whole place, you take pot-luck with your fellow guests - it can be a war-zone or the beginning of a beautiful friendship - but at least you know you all like snow.

The list below shows a selection of the companies offering chalet accommodation. The price brackets show an approximate figure per person for a week's holiday in mid season (including the cost of a flight).

budget (up to £500) - **skitotal**, **mountain discovery**, **crystal**

mid-range (£500-£800) **bigfoot, huski, esprit**

luxury (over £800) **collineige**, **flexiski**

privately run - information on these chalets is not as easy to find, although the internet is a good place to start - some owners have their own websites or list their chalets on other sites such as ifyouski.com. The Chamonix tourist office publishes a list of the private chalets available to rent for the upcoming season. Interhome also maintains a huge database of privately-owned accommodation and lists over 100 properties in the Chamonix valley.

What is on offer in privately run chalets varies greatly. Some provide a similar package to those run by tour companies, some are bed & breakfast only, and in some you are left entirely to your own devices.

apartments

The valley has a full range of apartments, from the small but functional to the large and luxurious. Half of Chamonix Sud is made up of apartment blocks, and there are others dotted around the town and valley. Be aware that large numbers of seasonnaires rent in Cham Sud, and in order to bring down the price per head there will often be four or more people living in a room designed for two.

An apartment for four is generally two rooms (a bedroom and living room), with two guests sleeping on a sofabed. On the face of it, they are the cheapest place to stay. But when you add in the price of food and meals out, you can pay more overall than you would pay for a hotel or chalet. However if you can live like a sardine and stay disciplined about what you spend on food, it can be cost-effective.

As with chalets, apartments can be found through the tourist office or through agencies in town. Some UK tour operators rent accommodation-only apartments.

Prices vary depending upon whether it is high, mid or low season. As a guide, a short-term let for a mid-grade apartment with two rooms (four beds) costs approximately €800 in high season and €300 in low season. Some apartments are available on a long-let if you want a place for the season. The demand is high so make sure you book early.

hotels

Each hotel has its own character and atmosphere, but they are often more impersonal than chalets and often the more you pay, the more formal the hotel will be - from the restaurant to the service throughout. You can book directly or through a tour operator. For reviews, see **hotels**.

onto the slopes

Once you have arrived in Chamonix and found where you are staying, there are a few things to do before you can get on to the snow. The following three sections will take you step by step through everything you need to know to get yourself on the slopes, from where and when to get your lift pass, through advice on ski, board and boot rental, to an overview of the options for ski schools and mountain guides.

snapshot

useful information

- no photo is needed for passes of 3 days or less.
- at peak times the queue for lift passes will be shorter at the Montenvers train station
- if you lose your pass, it's lost.
- it can be cheaper to buy your lift pass on a daily basis.
- there are discounts for under 12s, under 16s, families and over 60s.

lift passes

Buying a lift pass in Chamonix can be a complicated business. Though you can simply buy a standard pass for the number of days you are in resort, because of the way the ski areas operate, the more money conscious skier can save the price of lunch by being careful about what - or when - to buy.

chamski or mont-blanc?

There are two main types of ski pass available in the Chamonix valley - the ChamSki pass and the Mont-Blanc pass. The ChamSki pass is the standard, and gives access to the four ski areas, the Aiguille du Midi cable car, the Montenvers railway, and unlimited use of the Chamonix buses - pretty much everything you should want during your stay. The Mont-Blanc pass covers 10 resorts, and is something you are only likely to need if you are staying for a long time and have your own transport. The only potential drawback to the ChamSki pass is that it does not cover Les Houches - see **other resorts** in the **directory**.

In addition to everything covered above, a pass for 4 days or more allows you 1 day's skiing in Courmayeur (through the Mont Blanc tunnel in Italy - see **other resorts** in the **directory**). A 6 day pass also comes with two free '*tickets-top*', which you need to take the cable car from the Lognan mid-station to the top of the Grands Montets (see **les grands montets**).

While the ChamSki pass may be the most convenient - and ChamSki sales account for over 95% of passes sold to English skiers - if you have a specific agenda to ski certain areas, or if you are an absolute beginner, it may be worth looking into other options.

day passes

Morning, afternoon, and full-day passes for individual ski areas are available from the kiosks at the valley floor lift stations. If you are skiing 3 days and you ski 1 day in each of the three areas (for the single-day passes the Brévent and Flégère are considered one area) it works out cheaper to buy passes on a daily basis than to buy a 3 day ChamSki pass. This is because the ChamSki pass also gives access to the buses and to the Aiguille du Midi. In practice, if you are in ski gear you will never need to show a pass on the Chamonix bus - the significant difference is the Midi cable car, which is expensive without a ChamSki pass. But if you have no plans to ski the Vallée Blanche and are happy to miss out on the amazing view from the top of the Midi, buying single day passes may be the way to go.

beginners

If you are a complete beginner (the French word is *débutant*) and you expect to spend the majority of your time in the valley floor ski areas, you can buy a ChamStart pass, which will cover you just for those areas at a much lower price than the ChamSki. Extensions are available on a daily basis if you do decide to ski the main areas or if you want to meet friends on the mountain for lunch. For more details for complete beginners see **learning to ski**.

where to buy the passes

All the passes apart from season passes (see **seasonnaires** in the **directory**) are available from any of the valley floor lift stations (including the Aiguille du Midi cable car), from the tourist office, and from the Montenvers train station. The tourist office is the easiest place to buy them - it has the longest opening hours and the most proficient English speaking staff. The kiosk at the Montenvers station is a good option at busy times, as it's less known about and therefore less crowded. It also has very different opening hours: 9am-5pm with no break for lunch, as opposed to 8:30am-12:30pm and 2:30pm-7:30pm.

prices and discounts

The ChamSki pass is available for any number of days, and the longer the pass runs for the cheaper it is per day. The most common are the 3 and 6 day passes, for long weekends and week long holidays respectively. All sorts of deals are available, mostly aimed at families (see **children**), and it is worth reading the booklet on lift passes (available from the tourist office) or asking about offers when you buy your pass.

bad weather, accidents, lost and broken passes

If you are injured - and can produce a doctor's note - you can get a refund for the remains of a pass originally issued for 4 days or longer. Otherwise, the Compagnie du Mont-Blanc, who supply the passes and run the lifts, will not give you any kind of a refund for handing a pass back early. If you break your pass and can produce the remains, the tourist office will give you a replacement free of charge.

insurance

Insurance is not included as standard with lift passes, but it is available for a small daily supplement - you will be asked whether or not you want it when you buy your pass. If you have not organised your own already, the insurance on offer is highly recommended. It covers you for all on-piste incidents, including blood wagon and helicopter recovery.

skis, boots and boards

In spite of Chamonix being a town rather than a resort, it still feels as though every other shop is a ski rental shop (the French for rental is *location*). There are far too many shops to cover every one - what follows is an overview of ski and board rental and a brief description of some of the best places to go.

All of the stores employ either competent or native English speakers, and all the staff know enough English to fit you with the right skis and boots... as with most places trying a little French won't hurt, but unless you are a confident speaker this is one area where it's probably best to operate in a language you are comfortable with.

equipment and prices

Getting the right equipment will ensure you fully enjoy your holiday. Your feet will hurt if you don't get well-fitting boots so don't be embarrassed to persevere until you find a pair that fits. If your boots cause you problems after you have tested them out, take them back - all the shops will help you find a more suitable pair. Unless you know you want a specific type or make of ski, take the advice of the ski fitter. They are the experts and will know which is the best ski for you based on your ability and age.

skis

The majority of the rental places in Chamonix stock a decent range of skis. Rental prices do not vary much from shop to shop, so you may as well go to the one nearest to where you are staying - though some hotels and package holiday operators have deals with specific shops, usually for a 10% reduction on the rental price. If you want a specific brand of skis, you may have to hunt a little - most places carry Rossignol, Salomon and Dynastar but Atomics and some lesser known brands like Völkls are generally only found in the larger stores.

boards

Renting a board is very different from renting skis. While most ski shops stock some boards and boots, they are generally old, poorly maintained and of no use to anyone except absolute beginners. If you want decent equipment, a specialist boarding shop is the place to go - also because the people serving you are likely to be boarders, so will have more of an idea what they are giving you. Chamonix has five boarding-specific shops.

insurance & security

At most shops you can take out insurance (except on test skis) to cover accidental breakage, loss or theft. Unfortunately skis do get stolen or taken by accident - with so many people skiing on similar skis it's easy to confuse yours with those belonging to somebody else. When you stop for lunch or après, it's a good idea to swap one of your skis with a friend so you both have a mis-matched pair. This helps ensure that nobody will pick up your skis, either by mistake or otherwise.

individual shops

skis

ravanel & co (**valley c3**) is a Salomon specialist based in Les Praz, in the car park by the Flégère lift. If you're staying in Chamonix it isn't worth heading out, as you can find Salomon skis in most rental places in town, but if you're in Les Praz this is probably the best of the small selection of rental shops. They also carry Salomon snowboards.

sanglard (**town e3**) is a bit of a tardis - in spite of the small front, it is on three levels and carries an extensive range of outdoor clothing and equipment. Everything is well maintained, the staff know their stuff, and unlike most of the larger stores it is not a chain.

snell (**town d4**) is possibly the largest outdoor store in Chamonix, and stocks a huge range of specialist clothing, footwear and equipment for almost any mountain pursuit. It also has a substantial rental section and employs enough staff to start a small army.

sport 2000 (**town e2**) on Rue de la Gare just down from Chambre Neuf is a Rossignol specialist. The skis are very well maintained, the staff are friendly and professional people and the always-busy service shop out of the back of the store ensures all the skis are kept in excellent condition.

twinner (**town c4**) is a big chain of stores with two in Cham Sud, two in the town centre and one in Argentière. They carry most brands of skis, and a wide range of outdoor clothing and accessories. They employ knowledgeable staff, and the equipment is well serviced and reliable.

boards

invasion (**town f4**) is just out of the north end of town, across the road from the hotel Alpina. It is run by an Englishman, and although it is relatively new it is probably the best in town as regards quality and personal service. They have a wide range of new boards to rent and will set up whatever bindings you want. They also stock Invasion clothing and there is a printing room in the store where you can get your own designs put onto a t-shirt or car sticker.

otavalo (**town f4**) on the north edge of town is a specialist boarding and telemarking shop. All the boards have Flow bindings and they are all well serviced and in decent condition. Otavalo is French run and it's a good idea to have a go with whatever French you have.

zero-g (**town c4**) has a sales shop and a rental place that also sells last season's equipment at discount prices. French-run, all staff are riders themselves, and while the rental place feels a bit like a Poundsaver, the equipment and service are good.

trajectoire (**town c4**) is another Flow specialist, small and very well run with a good selection of boards to rent or buy. The staff speak excellent English and are both friendly and very enthusiastic about their sport.

other equipment

Rental shops offer a lot more than just skis and boards. You can hire touring skis, telemarks, snowblades, avalanche transceivers, snowshoes... in fact more or less anything you might conceivably need or want for the outdoors. The more specialist your requirement, the more likely you are to have to go to a large store - like Twinner, Snell or Sanglard - to find it.

ski school

Chamonix is entirely dominated by the ESF (*Ecole de Ski Français*), and while there are other ski schools operating they are all primarily guiding companies, with the exception of Evolution 2's Panda Club, a children's ski school based in Argentière.

esf

chamonix
t 0450 53 22 57
f 0450 53 65 30
e infoski@esf-chamonix.com
i esf.net/chamonix
office town e4 (maison de la montagne) - 8:15am-7pm

argentière
t 0450 54 00 12
f 0450 54 10 90
e esf-argentiere@wanadoo.fr
i esf-argentiere-valledechamonix.com
office argentière map e3
8:30am-12pm, 3pm-7pm

Chamonix is the centre of the ESF, and red-jacketed Frenchmen abound - especially during school holidays when there are up to 300 *moniteurs* (instructors) in resort. It is the oldest ski school in the Alps, and becoming an instructor is a difficult enough process that you are guaranteed a quality skier as your teacher. What you are not guaranteed is that you will be taught the latest techniques - older instructors who themselves learned on older skis may not be entirely up to speed on carving. It has been said that there as many ways to ski as there are ESF instructors. On the other side of the coin, many of the younger *moniteurs* teach both skiing and snowboarding, and there are charismatic and competent teachers in abundance.

Chamonix is a challenging place to ski no matter what your level of ability, and the ESF offers instruction to suit all levels. You will not so much see trains of youngsters zig-zagging down the slopes as you will see groups of boarders perfecting 360s and skiers working their turns on a slalom course. Even experts will find new things to try - though for that you are better off employing a guide (see **mountain guides**).

On the whole, the ESF is a very reliable and high quality establishment which suffers only from having such an enormous number of teachers on its books that you can never be sure that yours will be the best they have to offer.

group lessons
The cheapest way to take lessons is to join a group. You judge your own level of ability, to put yourself in group with a similar standard to yours. Your ability level is defined

either by the colour of run you are comfortable skiing on, or on your own assessment on your standard of skiing. In practice the divisions are not quite as accurate as they could be, as some people overestimate their ability or misunderstand words like 'confident' and 'controlled', so to an extent the level of your group is pot luck. But as long as you can distinguish whether you are a beginner, an intermediate, or an advanced skier or boarder you are likely to find yourself in roughly the right place.

private lessons

If you have the money, private lessons are without question the way forward. Once you're past the basics, individual attention is really the only way to make significant improvements to your technique, and is far better value for money than simply following an instructor around all day. If you are in a group of four or more the price is not much different to taking group lessons, and you can be guaranteed that you will go where you want to go and practise what you want to practise.

children

You can book lessons for children aged 4 years or over - see **children**.

lesson length

A half-day lesson (group or private) runs 8:45am-12pm, an afternoon lesson (private) runs 1pm-4:30pm, and a full day (private) runs 8:45am-4:30pm - with an implied break for lunch. If you book a private lesson and don't fancy the early morning start, you can of course ask for the lesson to start later - but the finish times will not change accordingly.

bookings

The easiest way to book is over the phone, as the office can become very busy and if you go in at the wrong time you'll probably find yourself standing in a long queue. On the other side of the coin, communication is always easier in person - and if you are taking group lessons you will have to go in at some point to pick up your lesson ticket (required in order to take the lesson). In peak season you should always pre-book, as there are not enough instructors to meet demand. To confirm your booking, the schools will need your name, level of ability and a credit card number.

cost

A half-day group lesson (ski or snowboard) will cost about €40, though you can get cheaper deals if you book multiple lessons. A half-day lesson with a private instructor costs around €135, and a full-day €225 - with the implication that you will buy lunch into the bargain. Other companies that offer lessons charge much the same. The price does not include insurance or a lift pass. You can pay by cash or credit card.

meeting points

The rendezvous for morning group lessons is at 8:45am, either at the HQ outside the **maison de la montagne** (**town e4**) or the Cham Sud main bus stop (**town a3/4**). Where the instruction takes place is rarely decided until the morning of the lesson, and will depend on snow conditions and on the make-up of the group. The Chamonix Bus runs a special ESF service to take group lessons to the slopes - but at lunchtime when you finish you're on your own. If you book a private instructor you can arrange whatever meeting point you like, and often if you meet at your accommodation your instructor will be able to take you to the slopes either by car or in an ESF minibus.

instructors

It is illegal to teach in France without a qualification recognised by the French establishment. In effect this means that the majority of instructors in France are French, as few other 'international' qualifications are accepted and the *equivalence* race test that foreign instructors must pass is extremely difficult. But this approach gives you the advantage of knowing that your instructor is at the least a very competent skier or boarder.

language

Almost all ESF *moniteurs* speak excellent English and there are also instructors who speak every other language - though you will need to book a long way in advance should you want instruction in a language less common to the Alps.

refunds and cancellations

Lessons take place whatever the weather, unless the entire lift system is closed in which case the ESF will refund the full lesson price. If you are ill or have an accident and can produce a valid medical certificate, they will also refund you. The ESF will refund a lesson that is cancelled a day in advance. If you cancel on the morning of your lesson, your chances of getting a refund are approximately equal to how charming you can be when you ask for one.

other ski schools

There are no other ski schools in Chamonix. The guiding companies **evolution 2** and **ski sensations** offer instruction - mostly in private lessons - and Evolution 2 also has a children-specific section called the Panda Club (see **children**). If you have a fear of red jackets, details of the other companies can be found in **mountain guides** (over the page) and in the **directory**.

mountain guides

To experience everything Chamonix has to offer, you will need to hire a guide. The glaciated terrain away from the valley's pisted areas is life-threatening to the inexperienced - but a guide can make possible to the intermediate skier what even an expert would hesitate to try unaided.

guides vs instructors

The difference between guides and ski instructors is fundamental. Instructing is about 'how', and guiding is about 'where'. Ski instructors are not qualified to take you off-piste, and you should not ask them to. In contrast, the limiting factor with a mountain guide is your own ability. If you are competent enough they will take you anywhere you want to go.

what's on offer

Anything you can think of. Along with the Vallée Blanche, you can hire a guide to travel the Chamonix-Zermatt haute route, ski the Pas de Chevre, or simply to take you where the powder is. Some companies offer mountain safety courses, ski-touring courses, rock- and ice-climbing trips, snowshoe expeditions... the list is as long as the mountains are high. Along with private bookings, most companies run a regular group trip down the Vallée Blanche. They will also show you around the pistes - but don't expect them to be too excited about doing it.

guiding qualifications

There is no question of a guide's ability. Becoming a guide takes years, and requires an intimate knowledge of everything the mountains have to offer. While they are invariably expert skiers, first and foremost they are mountaineers: they have extensive experience of the procedure and practice of mountain rescue, are proficient rock and ice climbers, are competent and comfortable in all types of conditions... they are the very definition of safe hands.

the pros

In addition to their skills on the mountain, guides will provide you with all the extra equipment needed on a trip: avalanche transceivers, harnesses, ropes, ice axes, crampons... all this is included in the initial price. Also, for Vallée Blanche trips your guide will reserve a place on the cable car, leaving you with more time to get worried about the hike down the arête.

the cons

As with private lessons, the downside to hiring a guide is the price. A full day can cost up to €300 - but you are better off spending the money and coming back alive.

the companies

There are more guides working in Chamonix than in any other resort in the Alps, and as a result there are a number of choices when reserving a guide. Most guides are very impressive, so whoever you book with you are unlikely to be let down. For contact details see **guides** in the **directory**.

compagnie des guides

The original guiding company. Its members are taken solely from Chamonix's indigenous population, and along with in-depth local knowledge, guides from the Compagnie have an ingrown passion for the area. It is a very professional establishment that is both aware and proud of its traditions, and you can be sure that whoever your guide, you will receive top class service - though the jacket might spoil your colour-coordinated photos.

cham ex

A more far-reaching company than most - in addition to the regular excursions they offer a range of specialist courses and extended trips across the Alps and throughout the world. The Argentière based company is run by Russell Brice, who is as famous a mountaineer as you will find anywhere, and many guides who are well-known in the mountaineering community work for Cham Ex on a freelance basis.

evolution 2

Advertising itself as being young and dynamic, Evo 2 offers a tradition-free approach which feels rather more commercial than other companies. Anything requiring a guide is likely to be dynamic, and an old guide is a good guide... but though their 'different' approach may not be so different, the guides are just as capable and the service just as good. They also run a children's ski school, called the Panda Club (see **children**).

ski sensations

Sensations is a small team of guides who offer group ski lessons in three day courses, and much the same off-piste range as the larger companies, specializing in ice climbing, paragliding, and mountaineering. Their office hours are frustratingly short, so enquiries and bookings are best made over the phone, and a long time beforehand if you are planning a trip during high season.

independent guides

Some guides work largely without attachment to a particular company. They are more authentic mountain men than career guides, and most spend as much time doing their own climbing and mountaineering as they do working. Most of their business comes through word-of-mouth, and because they are not constrained by company guidelines they are the best place to go for unusual requests like ice-climbing by head-torch, or for a moonlight descent of the Vallée Blanche.

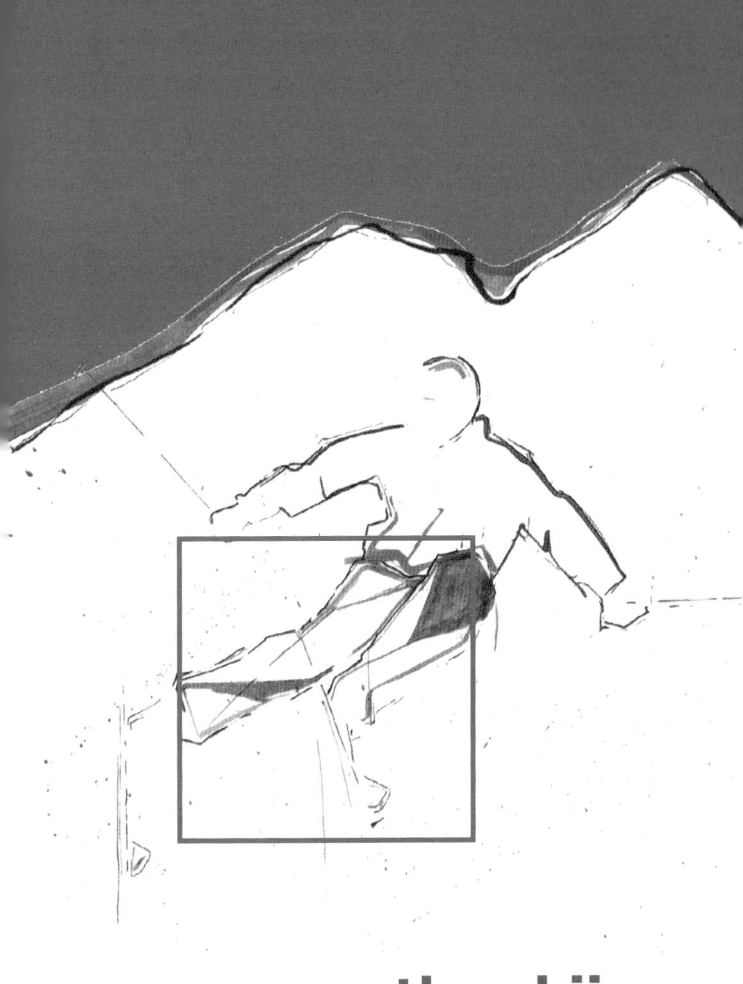

the skiing

the chamonix valley

Chamonix is a place to test your limits, and to extend them. The mountains offer a multitude of challenges to skier and boarder alike, but there are few enough easy runs that the faint-hearted will more than likely find themselves skiing the same stretch over and over. If you are willing, Chamonix will drag you out of your comfort zone - but if you are looking to cruise around within your envelope, you will probably be disappointed.

snapshot

- 150km of pistes - 7 greens, 20 blues, 17 reds & 9 blacks
- 36 lifts - 6 cable cars, 3 gondolas, 17 chairs & 10 drags
- off-piste - the vallée blanche & vast backcountry
- highest point - 3842m
- longest run - approx 22km

pistes

Considering Chamonix's enormous popularity, the number of pistes in the valley is surprisingly small. The total length of groomed runs is only 150km, so unlike huge areas such as the 3 Vallées or the Espace Killy, the Chamonix ski areas do not make for long day trips - if that is what you want, you will have to hire a guide and head off-piste.

The piste system follows the same colour-coding used in all ski areas throughout Europe - see under '**pistes**' in the **glossary**. Chamonix, though, has a higher than average proportion of steep runs. The blues are a little redder than in most resorts, and the reds a little blacker... the company on-piste is generally a little more aggressive too. In addition to this, you should only use the piste colour-coding as a general guide.

Although the gradient or width of each individual piste stays the same, other features such as snow conditions can change daily. A blue piste can become more testing than a nearby red, because it is over-crowded with skiers of ranging abilities or because of poor or icy conditions. And personal feelings about pistes vary greatly - an easy blue to one skier can seem like a vertical drop to another.

off-piste

The opportunities for off-piste skiing in the valley are almost unlimited. Apart from at Le Tour there are few marked itineraries, but there are a number of black runs which are unpisted and comparable to anything you might find in Verbier's 4 Vallées - and Chamonix's real off-piste is out of sight of any lift. Alongside and in between pistes in most areas you will find plenty of ungroomed snow on which to practise your off-piste technique without having to venture too far.

lifts

As with the pistes, the lifts are not about comfort. The resort is guaranteed popularity because of the excellent skiing, and for a long time the need to update the lifts was ignored. Recently the Compagnie du Mont-Blanc has begun a programme of refits - the liaison cable car between the Brévent and the Flégère has made a huge difference to skiing from Chamonix town, and the Bochard bubble on the Grands Montets is an efficient and welcome addition to the options from Lognan. There are plans to put in a lift connecting the small town of Vallorcine (out of the valley over the Col de Montets) to the Tête de Balme chair on the backside of Le Tour, and to drag the valley's older and less comfortable lifts into the 21st century... but it will be a gradual process, and for the time being there remains a mix of old and new.

Most of the lifts open from early December - the remainder being operational by about Christmas. The Brévent and Flégère are the first to close, around the middle of April, and Le Tour follows shortly afterwards. The lifts on the Grands Montets often run into early May, though the exact dates change yearly and if the snow conditions are good, the lifts may open earlier or close later than advertised. During shorter daylight hours in the depths of winter, the lifts close earlier in the day than later in the season when there is light until later. Opening and closing times are noted at the bottom of some lifts, or alternatively the tourist office will have full details of approximate times for the whole season.

the areas

The four ski areas are located as shown on the valley map (page 17). For each, you'll find a description of how to get to and from the slopes, the general characteristics and aspect of the area, and detail of the pistes, the off-piste, the mountain restaurants (denoted by the symbol ■) and where relevant, the local après. There is also a more detailed table of lift information and a piste map for each area (in which the piste colours correspond to those used by the resort). An explanation of how to use the lift tables and the maps is on the inside of the back cover.

where to go

beginners

Thousands of people of all ages choose to learn in Chamonix. In many ways it is the ideal place for beginners, in spite of perceived difficulties and the widely held belief that learning in Chamonix is a bad idea. It is true that there are few gentle slopes in the valley, and that because of the detached ski areas a lunchtime rendezvous between learners and non-learners needs prior planning. But the reality is that it is perfectly possible to learn here, and thanks to the ChamStart pass (see **lift passes**) it can be far cheaper for absolute beginners to learn in Chamonix than anywhere else - see **learning to ski**, on the facing page.

intermediates

If you are looking to push yourself to the next level, Chamonix is the ideal place to do it. The Brévent and Flégère have a variety of red runs and all of the Grands Montets is challenging: unless you spend all your time at Le Tour, you are likely to have to work pretty hard on many of the runs. If you want to improve your technique on moguls, the Grands Montets has a limitless choice, some of which is relatively gentle. For powder practice, the Brévent and Flégère have good variety but Le Tour has the most open space that isn't too steep.

experts

You will not want for adventure in Chamonix. The pistes will test you and dare you to go faster, and the off-piste will amaze you, scare you, and remind you who's in charge. All four ski areas have something for the expert, and away from the pistes there is no limit to what is on offer - the only downside is that to fully appreciate the valley you will need to hire a guide, partly because a wrong turn can put you in a lot of danger and partly because unless you really know the area, without one you are unlikely to find the best of what there is.

boarders

For most aspects of boarding, Chamonix is superb. The steep slopes make a great place to learn or to hone your technique, and there are abundant hits and lips in the natural terrain. All but two or three runs can be accessed without taking a draglift. The only thing lacking is a snowpark - the reality of the 'natural half-pipe' at Le Tour is a little disappointing, and the official park on the Grands Montets is ignored for the majority of the season - only being groomed for events like the ChamJam. But jumps and rails aside, it is difficult to think of a better destination to push you to the limits of your ability and beyond.

non-skiers

The main attraction for non-skiers is the Aiguille du Midi. For those unwilling to brave the Midi cable car the view from the top of the Brévent is an impressive - though utterly incomparable - alternative. As far as mountain walks go, though there are endless trails in the valley there is little provision for non-skiers in the four pisted areas.

learning to ski

If you have never worn plastic boots or strapped yourself to a plank of wood, the valley has four learners' areas which are gentle and unthreatening places to start. They can get very busy, but away from the main ski areas you are not constantly worrying about faster skiers shooting past and knocking you over - and the lift pass is much cheaper.

le savoy

A very gentle slope that isn't very wide so when busy it's like trying to ski to the toilets in a crowded pub. It is, however, an excellent location for children, as it's right in the middle of town. The top of the slope is next to the Brévent gondola, so people use the drag lift to avoid walking up the hill in the mornings - at 9am it can be amazingly busy. There is a small buvette which sells drinks, crêpes, and the like.

les planards

On the other side of town to Le Savoy, Les Planards is for those who are a step up the ability ladder. It provides an introduction to chairlifts, and two runs - a gentle blue through the trees and a straight but rather narrow red. Les Planards is also the end of the run down from the Vallée Blanche, so from midday onwards you'll see parties with harnesses and ropes and big smiles skiing down or eating in the Luge d'Eté restaurant. It tends to be less busy in the morning than other valley floor slopes, but this is for a reason - until the sun gets there around midday, it can be very cold.

les chosalets

Two gentle runs a short walk away from the Grands Montets cable car. Les Chosalets is to Argentière what Le Savoy is to Chamonix - a good spot for children and absolute beginners.

la vormaine

Higher up the valley alongside the Le Tour gondola, La Vormaine has snow earlier - and later - than slopes lower down. It gets busy, but it is a large and very open space, with either two or three runs depending on how it's pisted. Often one run is left ungroomed as a powder practice area. It is the ideal place to learn, as there is little difference between the runs at La Vormaine and the gentle blues higher up the mountain at Le Tour, so when you feel you're ready to progress you need only walk to the gondola station and head on up.

le brévent map p.65

The only ski area directly accessible from Chamonix town, the Brévent has something for everyone: gentle pistes for beginners and intermediates to practise on; fast and challenging reds and blacks for the more advanced; narrow couloirs and wide powder bowls for those in search of untracked powder. It also boasts awe inspiring views of Mont Blanc and the Aiguille du Midi, and with the cable car link to the Flégère the combined pisted area is the largest in the valley.

snapshot

- highest point - 2500m
- aspect - s & se
- access - gondola, cable car liaison with la flégère
- lifts - 1 cable car, 5 chairs & 2 drags
- pistes - 1 green, 5 blue, 3 red & 2 black
- off-piste - couloirs, bowls
- restaurants - 3

getting there

to the base station

on foot - the gondola station is a short walk from the centre of town - but it's a short very steep walk, so the best way to get there is to head to the Savoy nursery slope and take the draglift, which takes you to just above the base of the gondola.

by car - for a small hourly charge you can park in the multi-storey just above the gondola, which will have spaces even in peak season.

up the mountain - the Brévent has the most efficient base station, and queues rarely last long. At 9am the line moves more slowly because the ESF classes take priority, and when the resort is busy - or when the Flégère cable car is closed due to high wind - expect to wait up to a half hour.

aspect

Stretching above Chamonix on the north side of the valley, the slopes of the Brévent face predominantly south and south-east. By mid-afternoon the Brévent peak obscures the sun on some pistes (notably the Charles Bozon - the black from the top of the Brévent cable car), but the majority of the area catches the sun for most of the day.

the pistes

green - there is one short green run from the top of the Parsa chair, also accessible from the Altitude 2000 chairlift. It has its own easy draglift, and there is almost no high speed traffic so it is an unthreatening - and sunny - place to learn.

blue - with the exception of the initial green stretch that runs under the lift, all of the runs down from the Parsa chair are blues of varying gradients. They are only loosely marked as pistes - you can pretty much choose where you go and the area is large enough to keep you entertained for quite a while - with a few natural rollers and lips for the more adventurous. Elsewhere, from the top of La Source and La Charlanon, the blue track leading back to the Cornu chairlift is narrow but rarely busy, so it's not a bad place to practise away from the traffic.

red - for anyone of intermediate level or above a major highlight is the Cornu chair, which leads to two excellent red runs - a wide and sweeping piste back down to the bottom of the lift and a sustained slope off the back that leads towards the Flégère liaison. Conditions are consistently good throughout most of the day and both are varied enough to be skied again and again. For those graduating from blues, the two reds down the the Charlanon chair are almost always quiet, and have short steep sections that are ideal for getting in a few turns without getting out of control.

black - the Charles Bozon run from the top of the cable car is the best known of all the pistes on the Brévent. Though quite short it is very fast, and in the middle section you have the option of skiing one of the steepest mogul fields in the valley. The snow surface tends to be icy in the early morning, and by mid-afternoon there will be flat-light on the top section as the sun is obscured by the Brévent peak. There can also be lengthy queues for the cable car - the best times to go are late morning or over lunch when everyone else is tucking in to steak and chips. The only other black is accessed from the back of the Cornu chair - as the red piste bends right and becomes a track, straight down is a short, steep run that tends to be mogulled by the afternoon, and towards the end of the season will be slushy by lunchtime.

off-piste

There is extensive off-piste from the top of the Brévent cable car - as long as you know where you're going. Under the Cornu chair are two narrow couloirs which make for good practice with easy access. For an introduction to powder, a bumpy traverse to the right of the main Cornu piste followed by a short climb leads you to a wide bowl where the fresh snow doesn't get tracked out as fast as most places. It is also possible to make your way over to the Flégère without taking the liaison cable car, by climbing up from the top of the Cornu, then by way of the Col de la Glière down to the Combe Lachenal - but depending on the snow cover this will involve some hiking/skinning/snowshoeing, and the drop-in to the Combe de la Glière is a 35°-40° slope.

lunch

1 altitude 2000
t 0450 53 15 58

Reached by the Alt 2000 or La Parsa chairlifts, Altitude 2000 is a large and very busy restaurant with a decent menu of snacks, pizzas, full-blown meals and overgrown desserts. Service is not high-speed, but the food when it arrives will be more than enough to satisfy the appetite you work up while you wait. It's a little more expensive than the Brévent's other two restaurants, presumably because it is slightly more accessible and has a large outdoor section with a wind-break.

2 la bergerie
t 0450 53 05 42

At the top of the gondola, La Bergerie is probably the best the Brévent has to offer. There is a table-service restaurant upstairs and a self-service counter on the lower floor. The restaurant is fine, service is efficient and friendly and the self-service section is the only place on the Brévent where you don't have to wait around for someone to bring you your food. There are terraces on both levels, and the huge tartiflette pan is enough to make anyone's mouth water. The only let down is the hot drinks, which are served in tiny polystyrene cups that barely hold enough to satisfy a small mouse.

3 le panoramic
t 0450 53 44 11

At the top of the cable car, Le Panoramic is the place to go for great views. The higher you go the bigger Mont Blanc seems, and on a clear day the panorama out of the valley is fabulous (hence the name). The table service is generally slow, but the scenery makes the waiting much more bearable. You can take the cable car down again if you don't fancy the black run on a full stomach.

X picnics
None of the Brévent restaurants have picnic rooms. Probably the best places to pull out your thermos and unwrap your sandwiches are at the top of the Cornu chair and the top of the Brévent cable car (at the launching point for the Charles Bozon black run) - though this second area can get very busy with tourists.

getting home

on skis - the Nants run leads back to town from the bottom of the Parsa chair - and is an excellent way to avoid the afternoon queue for the gondola. It is marked on the map as a piste, but is groomed only once or twice a year, and is often closed due either to avalanche danger or rockfall. It is rated black thanks to a very steep top section, which becomes ledgy and nasty if there hasn't been snow for a while. After that, a winding track through the trees leads down to the gondola and the top of the Savoy nursery slope - allowing you to ski all the way into town if you want to.

by lift - when the resort is busy, even getting back to the gondola station can be a process - the four-man chair at La Parsa doesn't deal well with the traffic, and you may find yourself doing a lot of standing around. The queue for the gondola down will start to grow at about 3:30 in the afternoon. By 4pm there will probably be about a half-hour line - if you want to avoid queuing, head down at around 3pm or ski down (if the run is open).

après

From the gondola station it is only a 5 minute walk to the centre of town, but if you need a drink before heading down the hill - or if you are waiting to meet someone - a small bar just along the road provides the perfect spot. La Cabolée becomes a restaurant in the evening, but from lunchtime onwards it is open for the usual après mix of vin chaud, beer, and a deliciously sweet hot chocolate. Head to the main road below the lift station, turn right, and it is 30 yards away, opposite the Savoyarde hotel.

bad weather

There aren't many options on the Brévent when the weather closes in. If it's snowing heavily, the chances are the whole area will be shut, and as the weather clears it will re-open gradually, with the Brévent cable car being the last thing to get going again. Often after a dump of fresh snow the Bergerie restaurant becomes very full of people waiting to catch the first cable car up... but if it's snowing you are probably better off heading elsewhere.

la flégère map p.67

There are only five lifts on the Flégère, but the total skiable area is surprisingly large and aside from a gentle lower section the runs are steep and challenging. It is a bit like a mini version of the Grands Montets, and is home to the Index, a wide and exposed mountain face accessed by the Darth Vader lift. You'll understand the name when you see it.

aspect

As with the Brévent, the majority of slopes face south and south-east - which is good for sun, but resulting in slushy spring snow in late season. Many of the Flégère's runs are quite exposed and conditions can be very cold when the wind is up.

getting there

to the base station

on foot - the Flégère is walking distance if you're staying in Les Praz, otherwise it's a bus journey.

by car - be careful as you enter the car park: the odd one way system takes you in on the left hand side, though a lot of people don't see the signs - or choose to ignore them. You have to cross back to the right hand side as you leave... the best advice is to be cautious. The car park is not as large as it seems and it fills up fast, so get there early.

snapshot

- highest point - 2490m
- aspect - s & se
- access - cable car, cable car liaison with le brévent
- lifts - 4 chairs & 1 drag
- pistes - 2 green, 2 blue, 5 red & 1 black
- off-piste - wide, steep, open
- restaurants - 3

up the mountain - in contrast with the efficiency of the Brévent, the Flégère's cable car system is slow, and worse it is often closed because of high winds - sometimes even when there's no noticeable wind on the valley floor. Queues can look deceptively short because they continue inside the cable car building, so if you can see a queue outside then you probably have a half hour wait. When it's busy it is just as fast to go to the Brévent and take the liaison cable car across - and this is the thing to do when the Flégère cable car is closed, as the skiing will probably still be open and you may find you have all the pistes to yourself.

pistes

green - there are two runs, both down to the right as you come out of the cable car. They are fed by a narrow track, which makes for bust-ups between beginners and faster skiers heading for the Chavanne.

blue - the blue run from the Index is basically just a track, and can be difficult to follow. It is useful as an access piste if you are looking for bumps or fresh powder, but the run itself is never wide enough to cruise. From the top of the Chavanne you will find a sustained blue which feels quite steep, and is an excellent place to practise your technique as it is rarely too busy. The run down to Les Evettes and the Brévent liaison is another simple track.

red - if you've ever skied down a red run and felt it should be black, you'll know what to expect from the Flégère. The Index lift, a three-man chair also known as the 'Darth Vader', leads to some outstanding runs: the face of the Index, back down underneath the lift, is as steep a red as you are likely to find. From the Floria drag behind the Index lift, you reach a very long red that runs all the way down to La Trappe. The highlight of the Index's options is perhaps the Combe Lachenal, the start of which is a short walk from the top of the lift. It is long, steep, wide, and sustained, and takes you all the way down to the Brévent liaison and Les Evettes chair.

black - though some of the reds blur the boundary, only one run is rated black - the initial section to the right as you head down from the Floria drag. It is a short and steep descent that then becomes a red for the lower section down to La Trappe.

off-piste

You don't have to hunt for powder on the Flégère - so much of the area is wide open and unpisted. There are plenty of options down from the Floria drag towards La Trappe, and if you want tree skiing then take the Evettes chair and head straight back down under the lift. The Flégère is also the launching point for a number of single day touring routes to Le Buet, just out of the head of the valley on the other side of the Col des Montets. See **ski touring**.

lunch

The Flégère doesn't have much to offer for lunch - in the cable car station there is a standard fare restaurant and bar, and just outside by the Index lift is a snack stop which plays a distracting mix of less-than-mainstream music. Away from the cable car there is only one option.

1 **la chavanne**
t 0450 53 06 13

Designed as a sun-trap, the Chavanne is basically just a snack bar, serving hot and cold sandwiches and baguettes. It is, however, well placed to catch the weather, and you'll need to be early or lucky to get a lounger on the sundeck.

X picnics

There are plenty of perfect spots by the side of the green runs down to La Trappe - or if you want spectacular views then you can't do better than the top of the Index, where you have a panorama starting from the 4122m Verte peak and the Drus above Argentière, across the jagged Aiguille de Chamonix range that leads to the Aiguille du Midi and Mont Blanc.

getting home

on skis - the run back down to Les Praz is a pleasant track through the trees with a more open area towards the bottom. In contrast to the runs higher up the mountain, it is rated black when it barely feels like a red. If it is open, it is by far the best way to get back down to town.

by lift - the inefficiency of the cable car means that there are often queues to get back down to Les Praz. They can be considerable in high season - and as with the journey up the mountain in the morning much of the queue is inside the building so don't be fooled just because you can't see a line. In windy conditions the cable car is often closed, so you may find that you have to take the liaison over to the Brévent and come down into Chamonix town - though if this is the case the Chamonix bus will run a special shuttle service back to the car park in Les Praz.

après

Les Praz does not have a busy après scene, but if you want food or a relaxing drink you have a number of choices. The Eden hotel (see **hotels**) has a bar and family room which are open all day. The Lanchers hotel has a cosy bar, and the Cabine restaurant by the golf course serves excellent food if you have more time to spare.

bad weather

While the cable car often closes in strong winds, when there is low visibility the Evettes chairlift is one of the few in the valley that remains open, and will be one of the first to re-open after a heavy fall. The piste it serves is a track, but straight back down under the lift is a wooded area which offers a short but sweet (and steep) combat ski.

les grands montets
map p.69

There is nothing forgiving about the the Grands Montets. If skiing is about steep stuff, fast stuff, bumps, and wide open ungroomed space, this is one of the best areas in the Alps, and probably the world. The runs are demanding even for the most able skier, and after a week without snowfall the entire mountain face looks like a mogul field. Even the beginners' slope is relatively steep. Along with the Vallée Blanche, the Grands Montets is why people come to the Chamonix valley.

snapshot

- highest point - 3233m
- aspect - n & nw
- access - cable car & chairlift
- lifts - 1 cable car, 5 chairs & 1 gondola
- pistes - 1 green, 4 blue, 2 red & 3 black
- off-piste - endless: wide, exposed, moguls, trees, glaciated
- restaurants - 5

getting there
to the base station

on foot - there is a pedestrian route to the cable car from the centre of Argentière - if you're any further afield your only option is the bus.

by car - the free car park is very large and not too well organised. If it's busy there will be security directing you to a space - but if it's busy you are best off parking close to the exit: come 5 o'clock there can be an enormous jam as hundreds of people try to leave at the same time, but if you are parked at the main-road end of the car park you will be able to saunter past all the frustrated drivers and head straight back to town. Alternatively you could park your car in Argentière (see **argentière** for more information).

up the mountain - you have two choices to get to the skiing. The cable car to the Lognan mid-station is the obvious route, but while it is perfectly efficient, queues can be very long and such is the popularity of the Grands Montets that even out of high season there can be a significant wait. As an alternative - if you can put up with the cold - the left-hand queue in the main valley floor station leads to the 11 minute Plan Joran chair-lift. The wait at the bottom is always shorter - along with the cold and the time it takes, when you get to the top you then have to take another lift before you can do any skiing. But if you want to avoid standing around, that's the way to do it.

aspect

The slopes of the Grands Montets face mostly north and north-west, and as a result have by far the best snow conditions in the valley. It is the first area to open at the start of the season, and the last to close - with lifts usually running well into May. It gets no sunshine before about 11am, and in the height of winter can be very cold indeed, especially at 3233m at the top of the Grands Montets cable car.

the pistes

green - while the beginners' slope that runs alongside the terrain park may technically be a green run, it is as steep as many a blue. Worse, it serves as the run-off for a number of other pistes, meaning it is in constant use by high-speed traffic heading back to Lognan. Not a place for the faint-hearted learner.

blue - there's not much true blue on the Grands Montets: the runs that are rated blue serve mainly as access to powder and bump runs. Don't go looking for long cruisy pistes, because you won't find them.

red - as an improving intermediate you have a variety of choices: short and simple run from Les Marmottons; long and winding from the Bochard bubble; the narrow run that feeds the mogul fields under the Herse chairlift... there is no shortage of steep space to ski.

black - the marking of blacks on the Grands Montets is a little misleading. The Chamois run from the Bochard bubble is intended as a mogul run, and the winding track is there only as a dropping-off point. More importantly, the famous runs from the top of the Grands Montets cable car (the Point de Vue and Les Pylons) are never groomed, so while they are marked and patrolled as pistes, the conditions are very variable. With fresh snow, the run back to Lognan will be pure powder - but if there hasn't been a fall in a while the entire distance is likely to unpleasantly mogulled. Whatever the conditions, it is worth the queue at the bottom and the bumps at the top simply to ski down alongside the Argentière glacier, a view comparable to anything on the Vallée Blanche.

The Grands Montets cable car has a permenent queue at the bottom. You will more than likely have to wait for 30 minutes or more before you head up. In addition to this you have to buy a ticket for every journey - available from the kiosk at the mid-station. See **lift passes**.

off-piste

The off-piste options are almost limitless, and in addition to the huge open spaces the Grands Montets is also home to the Glacier d'Argentière and the Pas de Chevre (see **off-piste**). For those simply wanting powder, the area is so large that even days after a fall there will be fresh tracks to be made somewhere. For bumps skiers, the routes between the pistes become mogulled very quickly, and unless there's been a heavy snowfall you can ski on nothing but bumps all day if you feel so inclined.

lunch

The Grands Montets has a number of choices for lunch. Of the restaurants covered below, Lognan and Plan Joran can be very busy and the others are somewhat out of the way - if you want to avoid the queues withhout risking getting lost, you can ski down to the base station, where there are two restaurants and a bar, all of which are perfectly acceptable.

1 lognan

t 0450 54 10 21

The mid-station has a large restaurant on two levels: downstairs is self-service, upstairs is very average table service. Outside there is a snack bar, and your best option may be to buy a *sandwiche mixte* and get in the queue for the cable car up. There are sun-loungers outside the restaurant section, where you can picnic if you want.

2 plan joran

t 0450 54 10 21

Considered by some the best mountain restaurant in the valley, and offering a far more ambitious menu than you will find anywhere else. The food is comparable to the better quality places in town - the difference comes in the speed of the table service, which as with most mountain restaurants can be painfully slow. But it does offer a superb range of cuisine and some mouth-watering desserts, and when it is good, it is very good.

3 chalet refuge de lognan

t 0660 16 86 33

Difficult to get to and even more difficult to get away from, the Chalet Refuge is not ideally placed. You reach it either from the bottom of the Point de Vue run (from the top of the Grands Montets cable car) or by traversing over from the top of the Herse chairlift. Either way you will have worked up an appetite by the time you arrive. It is a small and homely restaurant, away from the masses and with a beautiful view of the glacier. Be warned though - there is no piste leading away from the hut, so you will either have to hike back up the track you came down, or take on a tricky traverse down to the Lognan mid-station or to the red run back to Argentière.

4 snack bar 3300

Inventively named, this is a snack bar at the top of the Grands Montets cable car, attractive mainly because you can eat your lunch on the roof terrace. Great views, standard food.

5 **la crèmerie du glacier**
t 0450 54 07 52
An excellent and very out of the way restaurant, specialising in local food. By late season you can reach the Crèmerie by road, but when everything is still snow-covered it is more of a struggle to find. It lies to the right of the red run down to Argentière, at the bottom where the piste intersects with the cross-country route. But blink at the wrong moment and you'll miss it.

X **picnics**
As you come out of the Bochard bubble, hike up the spike that's straight in front of you. The view in any direction is fabulous, and right below you is a more-or-less sheer drop down to the Pas de Chevre. Few people venture up there, because it looks like the start of a scary off-piste run (it's not - though you could technically join the Pas de Chevre from here, you'd need very good snow cover and to be a very, very good skier). If you want to eat indoors, Plan Joran has a picnic room or you can eat outside on the loungers by the Lognan restaurant.

getting home

on skis - the red run down has good artificial snow cover, and is open until very late in the season. It can get extremely busy at the end of the day, and the whole run is an accident blackspot as all levels of skier and boarder make their way down what is at times quite a narrow piste. Nevertheless, it is better than taking the cable car, and is in no way difficult as red runs go.

by lift - the cable car will not be busy until the end of the season when you can no longer ski down. If you prefer, you can take the Plan Joran chair down to avoid whatever queue there might be.

après

Behind the cable car base station, at the bottom of the run down, there are two restaurants and a bar (with a live band every afternoon) - all of which are good quality. Away from the slopes, the town of Argentière has its own après scene - for more information see **argentière**.

bad weather

The Grands Montets gets more than its fair share of bad weather. Clouds seem to be attracted to the ski area, and often when the rest of the valley is in warm sunshine the Grands Montets will be in a white-out. The sun will usually break through by the afternoon, but until it does there's nothing much to do except wait - though the run back to the valley floor tends to stay below the clouds. The Grands Montets cable car is invariably the last lift to re-open after a fresh fall - leading to hordes of powder hounds camping out at the Lognan restaurant waiting to catch the first car up.

le tour map p.71

On rolling slopes at the head of the valley, Le Tour is the gentle alternative to the rest of the skiing in Chamonix. It is not, however, only for family cruising: much of the best powder and tree skiing is found there, and it is the least busy of the four areas by quite a stretch - though on weekends with the influx of locals it can still be pretty hectic.

getting there

to the base station

on foot - walking to Le Tour is not an option. Unless you are staying at the Olympique hotel by the gondola, or in the small town of Montroc, you're on the bus.

by car - it's about 15 minutes from Chamonix to Le Tour without traffic. At weekends the free car park will be full by 11am, and the overflow is more than a mile away - so get there early. In high season the journey back to Chamonix can take over 45 minutes in the rush hour, so head down early or take lots of sweets with you.

up the mountain - the gondola up to Charamillon is efficient and quieter than the other base station lifts. That is not to say that there are never queues, but they are less common and less long than elsewhere in the valley. From the top of the gondola, the Autannes chairlift provides access to the main skiing.

snapshot

- highest point - 2270m
- aspect - all
- access - gondola
- lifts - 2 chairs & 4 drags
- pistes - 9 blue, 5 red & 1 black
- off-piste - extensive: bowls, trees, itineraries to vallorcine & trient (switzerland)
- restaurants - 3

aspect

Being at the top of the valley, the slopes at Le Tour face in a variety of directions. The entire area is wide open and catches sunshine for much of the day, with the exception of the backside down to the Tête de Balme chair, which is mostly shaded by trees. Thanks to its higher bottom altitude, Le Tour spends longer above the snowline and so has better early and late season snow than the Brévent and the Flégère.

the pistes

green - there are no green runs on the mountain - though see La Vormaine in **learning to ski**.

blue - the gentle slopes of Le Tour make for a lot of cruisy blues. The majority of the slopes in the area are wide, rolling runs with lots of space for easy turns. One of the highlights of the area is the run leading down through the forest from the Tête de Balme chair to Vallorcine, on the other side of the Col des Montets - but be warned, there is currently no lift to take you back up again. To return to Le Tour you will have either to shuttle cars or take the hourly train to Montroc and catch the bus from there back to the bottom gondola.

red - as much as the reds feel black on the Flégère, they feel blue at Le Tour. There is nothing very steep or narrow in the whole area, and apart from the run down to the Tête de Balme chair, the few reds seem to be there simply to prevent monotony on the piste map. That said, the runs are fun and because of their width are a good place for beginners to improve or for the more advanced to find their ski legs.

black - one black run is marked on the piste map, but as with the runs from the top of the Grands Montets it is not actually pisted - it is simply a route down underneath the Tête de Balme chair, and it is a fine place to find powder and good tree-skiing.

off-piste

For anyone not looking for a relaxing day, the reason to go to Le Tour is to find powder. Because almost everyone who heads away from Chamonix after a snowfall goes to the Grands Montets, fresh snow gets skied out far less quickly at Le Tour. Various large powder bowls are clearly visible and require little or no hiking to reach. The itinerary routes back down to the car park hardly ever get touched, and there is a wealth of open terrain and tree-skiing off the pistes down to the Tête de Balme chair.

lunch

1 chalet de charamillon

t 0450 54 09 05

A large yet cosy restaurant, like Plan Joran with better views but without the fancy menu. There is a terrace, a large outdoor seating area, and a picnic room on the lower level.

2 col de balme refuge hut

t 0450 54 02 33

If you want something out of the way and completely different, the Col de Balme hut is your place. It is an authentic refuge, with scant décor, as-it-comes service and an outdoor hole-in-the-floor toilet. There is barely any choice on the menu, but the steak and chips is cheap, and tastes deliciously home-cooked. Also, it is at the end of a flat track - the effort it takes to reach means it doesn't attract the masses that fill most restaurants. The hut is on the Swiss border, and as well as Euros accepts Swiss Francs should you have any knocking around.

3 the snack-stop

On the red run from the Autannes lift back down to the gondola is a small snack bar which isn't marked on the official piste map, and which is easy to miss. As a result it rarely gets too busy, and though the food is simple (and heated in a microwave) it's a great place to sit on a sun-lounger and sip a vin chaud.

X picnics

The top of the Autannes chair has the best view of the valley - but it can be very windy. At the bottom of the Tête de Balme chair is a sheltered sun-trap which is probably the best spot on a windy day. No one will mind - or even notice - if you picnic at the snack-stop, or alternatively there is a picnic room in the Chalet de Charamillon.

getting home

on skis - the red run under the gondola is as unthreatening as the other reds at Le Tour, and is open right up to the end of the season. After a few broad turns you come to a long final schuss under the gondola that is a fantastic way to end your day's skiing.

by lift - if you don't fancy the ski down you can take the gondola. There is rarely - if ever - a queue to go down.

après

The bar at the Olympique hotel is small and cosy, and has a large terrace for sunny days. Aside from that the only option is the tiny *buvette* at La Vormaine, which is not cosy and which has a very small 'terrace' for sunny days - but which is usually considerably quieter.

bad weather

When it's windy anywhere in the valley, it's very windy at Le Tour - and therefore also very cold. The tree skiing down to the Tête de Balme chair would make Le Tour an excellent place to go in poor visibility, but more often than not the windspeed will close the access lifts and you won't be able to get there. In short, Le Tour is probably best avoided unless it's sunny.

off-piste

While the valley's pisted areas are steep and challenging, Chamonix's reputation comes almost entirely from its off-piste skiing. It boasts the justifiably renowned Vallée Blanche, much of the best known and most dangerous extreme skiing in the Alps, and is the launching point for numerous ski-tours including the original *haute route*. What follows is a description of some of Chamonix's better known routes - none of which should attempted without a guide. For a full description of Chamonix's off-piste see the dual-language book *Chamonix Hors-Piste*, by François Burnier and Dominique Potard, available from most bookstores in Chamonix.

the vallée blanche

Every year, people from all over the world come to Chamonix just to ski the Vallée Blanche. Its length varies depending on whose description you read, but at roughly 20km from the Aiguille du Midi back down to Chamonix, and with a vertical drop of almost 3000m, it is the longest lift-accessed glacier run in the world. The views are quite unforgettable, and there is skiing to suit all levels of ability from intermediate upwards. Anyone who is comfortable in a controlled snowplough turn can get down the classic route - for boarders accurate control of tight turns is required. The attraction is not how or what you are skiing, but where.

The Vallée Blanche has become something that skiers 'do' in the same way as tourists 'do' Paris or 'do' Rome. The scenery is quite astounding - aside from the hundreds of other skiers, it is an almost otherworldly experience. If you have never strayed out of sight of a lift or a piste marker before, you will not believe your eyes. The descent is on a vast expanse of snow between two towering lines of mountains, between seracs (huge blocks of glacial ice) and over snow-bridges that span deep crevasses. Aside from the Requin Hut halfway down (and ignoring all the other people), there is no sign of civilisation. For the recreational skier it is an experience you will never forget.

However, it is high-altitude glacier skiing, and it should not be approached lightly. People die on the Vallée Blanche every year - and almost all accidents happen because of poor preparation or overconfidence. Unless you are proficient on and well equipped for crevassed terrain, you must go with a guide.

getting ready

In the high mountain environment the weather can change from warm sunshine to freezing white-out in a matter of minutes. It can be as cold as -30°C on the Aiguille du Midi, and

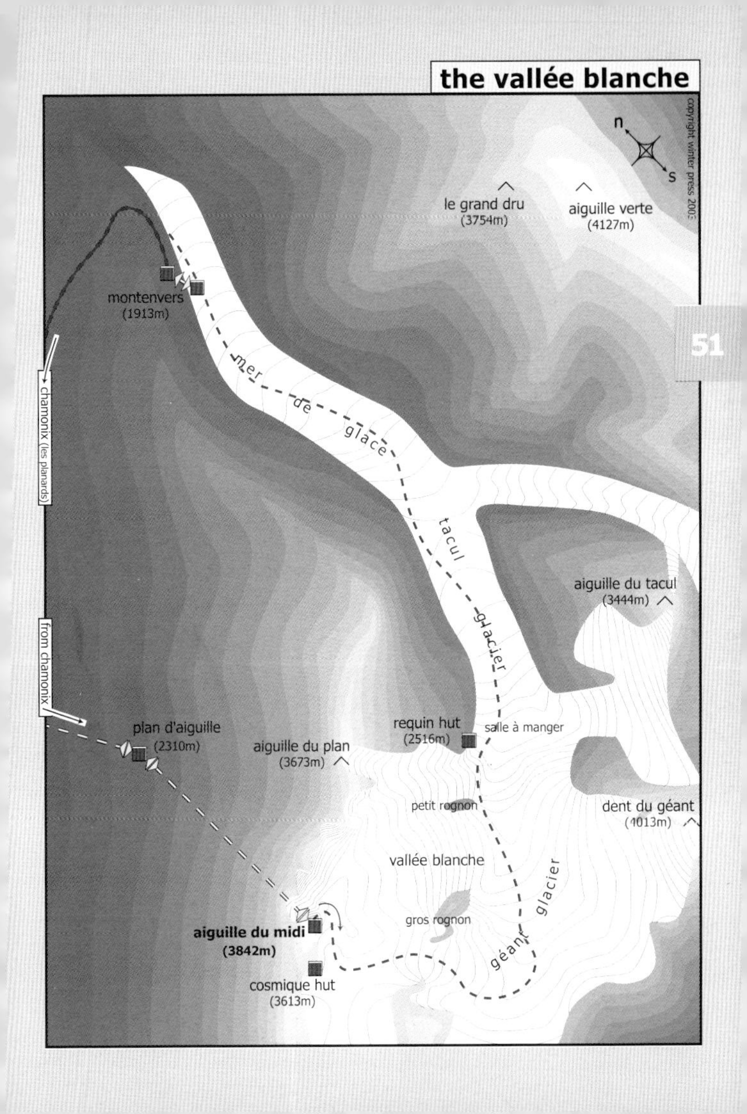

the vallée blanche
copyright winter press
n
s
le grand dru
(3754m)
aiguille verte
(4127m)
montenvers
(1913m)
chamonix (les planards)
mer de glace
tacul glacier
aiguille du tacul
(3444m)
from chamonix
plan d'aiguille
(2310m)
requin hut
(2516m)
salle à manger
aiguille du plan
(3673m)
petit rognon
dent du géant
(4013m)
vallée blanche
géant glacier
gros rognon
aiguille du midi
(3842m)
cosmique hut
(3613m)

sunshine down in town is no guarantee of good weather on the mountain. You should take a warm skiing hat, good gloves, goggles as well as sunglasses, a fleece to wear under your skiing clothes... you may need none of this, but better to bring it than to rue the decision not to. This is the first of a number of reasons to go with a backpack - though if you have never skied with one before, you should be aware that it significantly changes your centre of gravity and so until you adjust to it you may find your balance is a little off.

The Vallée Blanche is busy enough that you need to reserve places on the cable car if you want to ski it in the morning. Your guide will take care of this - you just need to remember your lift pass. If you are going without a guide, you can book either at the base of the cable car or through an automated telephone reservations line - see the **directory**.

food

You could get from top to bottom in 2 hours if you had to, but it is worth taking your time and you are likely to need to eat at some point. There is a restaurant at the top of the cable car, and the Requin Hut at the halfway stage sells food like any other mountain restaurant. But it is always jammed beyond capacity, and a lot of skiers carry sandwiches with them to eat on the way down. Just past the technical stretch through the Géant icefall (see below), the Salle à Manger (dining room) provides the perfect picnic spot. If you decide not to carry lunch, you would be well advised to carry at least a couple of chocolate bars and a bottle of water just in case. Even if you don't need them, someone else in your group might do.

safety equipment

In addition to warm clothing and food, you will need an avalanche transceiver and a climbing harness, and each group will need a rope. You ski the whole way down wearing your harness - it's very difficult to get someone out of a crevasse if they're not wearing one. Your guide will provide all the equipment and explain how to use it, and will also carry the rope, which is used on the arête (see below) and which would be used for a crevasse rescue.

the aiguille du midi

At the shoulder of Mont Blanc, the Aiguille du Midi stands 3842m high. There is little danger of suffering from altitude sickness at this height, but coming from ground level the air is thin enough to make you short of breath if you try to exercise - if you're sceptical then try running up the stairs to the terrace. Given what it is standing on, the construction is very impressive, and the views from the Midi alone are worth the trip - see **snow activities**.

the arête

The descent begins with the notorious hike down the arête - about 100m of stepping down a narrow path with a steep drop-off on one side and a very steep drop-off on the other. The north face of the Aiguille du Midi is a 45° convex slope - which gives you a humbling perspective on how shallow even black runs are by comparison. As you stand at the top of it, it feels like 60°. You may not believe it as you look down, but people ski off it.

If you are scared of heights, you won't like it much, but in reality it is not at all dangerous. People have fallen from the path - and if you fall unroped you are unlikely to survive - but if you are with a guide you will be wearing a climbing harness, and will be roped up to everyone else in your group - so if you slip you won't slip far. Conditions on the path are very variable, and when it's icy, ski boots don't grip very well. Boarders have it easier here, as the rubber soles of boarding boots cope a little better with ice. Wearing crampons makes this climb a simple walk - ask your guide the day before if you are at all concerned.

There is a rope on either side of the path to help you balance - but carrying skis and poles it can all become a bit of a panic, especially given the large numbers of people trying to get down at busy times. Another reason to bring a backpack is that if you can attach your skis or board to it, your hands will be much freer to help you climb down.

skis on!

Once you have cleared the arête you reach a small flat area where you can put on your skis or board. This is the launching point for every descent. Unless it has snowed recently, the initial section is likely to be unpleasantly mogulled, but after 50m or so the run flattens out and you are away. 95% of skiers take the classic route down the glacier - if you are in a group of very able skiers there are all sorts of other ways down that are more challenging, and which will have better snow and fewer people. A couple of minutes skiing will be enough for your guide to decide which route is best for you.

the classic route

On a clear day you will share the valley with hundreds of other skiers and boarders, and it can feel like a busy piste. The classic route is shown on the Vallée Blanche map as a dashed red line. Apart from crossing the Seracs du Géant, the whole descent is like a very wide blue run - but don't let this fool you into straying away from the path your guide takes. The entire run is on a glacier, and crevasses can be difficult to spot unless you know what you are looking for. You should never ski below your guide, nor more than ten yards or so either side of the route your guide takes. A simple bump may conceal a gaping hole.

the seracs du géant

About half-way down, the classic route meets the Géant icefall. This is the most impressive part of the descent, and the most challenging section of the skiing. It is basically like a nasty mogul field - it is not very steep, but the bumps are often ledgy. It is essential here that you follow your guide's tracks precisely, turning exactly where your guide turns. You are within feet of crevasses on either side, and you are skiing between huge blocks of glacial ice. Take your camera.

back to chamonix

After following the Mer de Glace down from the Salle à Manger, the return to town is either by skiing down to join the slopes of Les Planards, or by taking the Montenvers train. Skiing down involves climbing up from the tip of the Mer de Glace over the brow to a small *buvette* where you can buy food and drink, and then heading on down on a cat-track through the woods. It is narrow and winding, but flat enough to be a simple ski. If there is not enough snow you can take the Montenvers cable car up to the train station. You need your lift pass to use the train.

guides on the vallée blanche

Most Chamonix guides get most of their business from taking groups down the Vallée Blanche, and for them the classic route can become monotonous. If you simply want to ski, just follow your guide down the hill. But if you have any interest in your surroundings, your guide will know the area inside out. If you want to see a huge crevasse from a safe distance, or if you want to know anything about off-piste skiing, most guides will be more than happy to oblige. Similarly if there is anything you are uncomfortable with, just ask - on the whole they are a very friendly and approachable bunch. See **mountain guides**.

for boarders

On the classic route there are long flat sections where you may run out of speed, especially if there is a lot of fresh powder. Though you probably won't need them, it is a good idea to take hiking poles or ski poles so you can help yourself along - another good reason to take a backpack. This is especially true if the other people in your group are skiers, as they will probably stop on sections where it will be difficult for you to pick up speed. If you are unsure, ask your guide before you leave.

beating the crowds

The Vallée Blanche is such an attraction that it is likely to be very busy even during low season. You will not catch the first lift by getting there early in the morning - by 7:30am the cable car station is heaving with skiers, climbers and mountaineers. There are ways to avoid the crowds - but they require a bit of forward planning. One way is to take the last cable car up in the afternoon (at about 4pm) and to stay the night in the Cosmiques Hut, a short traverse from the Aiguille du Midi. The views of the sunset are extraordinary, and staying in a mountain refuge hut is an experience in itself. The following morning you can head down the glacier in perfect quiet, with just the morning sun to keep you company. One word of warning though - sleeping at altitude and thus in thinner air often affects how easily people sleep, so your night's rest may not be entirely restful.

other options

If the arête isn't your cup of tea, or if you want to avoid the queuing before you even get onto the cable car, it is also possible to ski the Vallée Blanche from the Italian side. Through the Mont Blanc tunnel you can reach the base station in little over 20 minutes, and there is rarely much of a queue at the bottom of the lift. There is no arête to hike, the top section of the skiing is likely to have much better snow conditions, and you can enjoy an authentic Italian pasta lunch at the mid-station restaurant before you leave. Just remember your Gucci sunglasses.

glacier d'argentière

If you've ever seen it, you'll know that not much skiing takes place actually on the Argentière glacier. It is an extraordinary series of gaping crevasses, and is much better looked at than stepped on. Skiing is possible alongside the glacier - the Point de Vue run from the top of the Grands Montets cable car takes you within spitting distance of the lower section, and with a guide you can descend straight down to the glacier and ski along the left bank, or take various other routes down away from the piste markers.

the pas de chevre

Often fondly mistranslated as the 'No Goats', the Goat Step is a steep and scary couloir descent, which you can't opt out of once you have started. Don't even consider the Pas de Chevre unless you are an expert skier, and no matter how good you are don't try it without a guide. There are three couloirs from the top of the Grands Montets cable car west down to the Mer de Glace. They are all steep, and they are all technically very demanding. Route finding in the bottom section can be extremely difficult if there is poor snow cover. But if you have the ability, and the guts, the Pas de Chevre will be one of the experiences of your life.

ski touring

There is a whole world of skiing that goes almost unnoticed by the majority of recreational skiers. Those used to huge, linked ski areas with endless lifts and mile after mile of pisted runs may well not know what ski touring is. It is also called ski mountaineering, which is perhaps a more appropriate name for it - it consists effectively of climbing up mountains before skiing down them. It is quite unlike normal skiing in that it is entirely off-piste, and 'tours' consist of travelling from 'a' to 'b' in the same way as hiking trails in summer.

Obviously to make this possible a lot of different equipment is necessary. To climb up slopes with skis on you need touring bindings, which you can unlock to allow your heel to come away from the ski as you step upwards. You also carry 'skins' - so called because they were originally seal skins - which are strips attached to the bottom of the ski during a climb to allow them to slip uphill but prevent them from sliding down. For many tours it is also necessary to be proficient with climbing ropes and harnesses... but as with most things in Chamonix, if you hire a guide you will be surprised what you can do - and all these delights are available to boarders as well, simply using snowshoes or approach skis when skiers use skins.

starting off

Chamonix is the perfect place to start ski touring - and few people that try it ever look at piste skiing in the same way again. A short route from the top of the Cornu lift (in the Brévent area) via the Col de la Glière down to the Combe Lachenal (in the Flégère area) combines a good introduction to skinning with a short but sweet powder run.

An excellent start to true touring is the mini-tour over the Col de Berard. The route starts on the Flégère and finishes in the small town of Le Buet, out of the top of the valley on the other side of the Col de Montets. The first half of the tour involves an hour or two of hiking and skinning, split into two sections by a 10 minute traverse. The second half is a beautiful 1-2 hour descent from the Col de Berard along the line of the Eau de Berard river, which by mid April will be melted and flowing. You are unlikely to see many other people, as the tour is a way off the beaten track. From Le Buet there is an hourly train service back to Chamonix - the station is just over the road from the hotel and bar where the tour ends. The best map that covers the route is the IGN (the French OS) hiking map number 3630OT, a 1:25000 scale topographical map available from any of the bookstores in town.

the haute route

The 'high level road' from Chamonix to Zermatt takes 6 days to complete, crossing more than 20 glaciers and with some 10000m of combined ascent and descent. It was first skied in the early 20th century, and though many other haute routes have since been established this is the original, now known as the 'classic' haute route.

The route can of course be done in reverse, from Zermatt to Chamonix, but the majority of parties travel from west to east, starting above Argentière at the top of the Grands Montets cable car, and via a number of variations finishing in Zermatt under the north face of the Matterhorn. The nights are spent in refuge huts - small buildings dotted around the mountains which provide evening meals, basic sleeping space, and an escape from cold and inclement weather.

It will make very real demands on your skiing and on your personal fitness, and it should not be undertaken without considerable preparation. The reward is outstanding skiing in some of the most beautiful mountain scenery in the world, making your way through high-alpine backcountry from Mont Blanc to the Matterhorn. Europe's mountains offer nothing better.

For a full description of the route, see Peter Cliff's book *The Haute Route*, published by Cordee and available from most bookstores in Chamonix.

suggested days

If the weather isn't doing you any favours, or if you need some ideas about where to head for something specific, below is a bit of location advice.

the first morning

While the valley's most gentle slopes are at Le Tour, you probably don't want to spend your first morning (and your first evening) stuffed in a bus. Save the journey up the valley for the middle of the week - when there will be fewer people - and get your ski legs back on the Brévent, which has plenty of wide blue space and enough variety for you to build up your confidence without getting bored.

in poor snow

When there's not much skiing to be done, head for the Grands Montets. It is the highest of the four areas, and the north facing slopes hold the snow for longer than anywhere else in the valley. The pistes are the first to open at the start of the season, and the last to close - normally staying open into early May. If it's the middle of the season and hasn't snowed for a long time, most of the area is likely to be very much a mogul field, but the pistes will still be pistes, and while the snow may be icy in the morning and/or slushy in the afternoon, anything is better than no snow at all.

in bad weather

When the weather closes in, the ChamSki pass has little to offer. One or two of the lower lifts on the Flégère may be open, but basically in poor visibility there's not much to be done. If you must have a day's skiing, Les Houches at the bottom of the valley is under the tree-line, as is Italy's Courmayeur, just the other side of the Mont Blanc tunnel and closer than you might think. However, Les Houches is only covered by the Mont-Blanc pass, and though a ChamSki pass of 4 days (or longer) gives you a free day in Courmayeur, the tunnel will set you back €40 just to get there. See **other resorts**.

a good lunch

While the Col de Balme refuge hut at Le Tour is an interesting experience, the only place you'll find memorable food on the mountain is on the Grands Montets. Plan Joran offers an excellent menu and some mouth-watering desserts if you don't mind waiting for your meal, or if you're feeling adventurous the Chalet Refuge de Lognan serves good food and is away from the pistes in the shadow of the Argentière glacier - but it takes a bit of getting back from. For something that takes a bit of getting to, the Cremèrie du Glacier serves perhaps the most hearty (and non-touristy) lunch available - if you can find it. See **les grands montets** for all of these restaurants.

a mid-week change of pace

If there's been a fresh snowfall, or if after 3 or 4 days your enthusiasm for steeps and moguls is starting to wane, a day at Le Tour can provide the perfect antidote. You will be hard pressed to find a single bump in the whole area, and most of the pistes are wide and gentle. There are great views back down the valley to Chamonix, some beautiful runs through the trees down to the Tête de Balme chair and Vallorcine, and lunch is available from - amongst other places - an authentic refuge hut, which is a far cry from your standard mountain restaurant.

a bumpy ride

If you like your moguls, the Grands Montets is unbeatable. The top cable car leads to the famous Point de Vue and Pylons runs, neither of which are pisted and both of which, unless there is fresh powder, will be mogulled for almost their entire length. They are both steep and sustained descents, and there is no backing out once you've started - but if that doesn't sound like you, the Grands Montets also has moguls to suit every other appetite. The Chamois black run from the Bochard bubble is steep but has a relief track, and the whole area gets skied so much that everywhere on the mountain there are bump runs, of varying gradients and so suited to varying ability levels.

one for the kids?

Because the valley's pisted areas are unlinked there may well not be enough variety to keep the more discerning child entertained for a whole day - and unless your children are competent skiers, there is little to recommend away from Le Tour. As for the Vallée Blanche, youngsters are often unimpressed by its beauty - especially if they've lost their sense of humour on the arête - and queues to get there and to get back probably won't go down too well with anyone who has got a short attention span. Not an easy choice.

to get away from it all

Even when the resort isn't too busy, the valley's pisted areas are small enough that escaping for a bit of peace and quiet can be a difficult thing to do. If you want to see a mountainside that isn't covered in skiers, the best thing to do is to go ski-touring. Hire a guide to take you on the mini-tour over the Col de Berard and down to Le Buet, and the chances are you will barely see another group for most of the day. To do this, however, you need to be a competent skier (comfortable on black runs or off-piste), you need to be in reasonable physical shape, and you'll need to hire touring skis. If you're a boarder, the same trip is possible, using snowshoes where a skier would use skins. See **ski touring**.

events

Chamonix is home to a number of world-class winter events. The jagged mountains provide the perfect forum for extreme competitions, and the Grands Montets snowpark is home to the best known freestyle competition in the Alps. There are also a number of smaller events that are not swamped by professionals - so if you've perfected that 360 and fancy your chances, read on...

the chamjam

A week long jamboree of competitions and parties, the ChamJam is famous throughout the world and is responsible for Chamonix's busiest week of the season. It attracts huge media coverage (for a skiing and boarding contest), there is invariably some scandal or other during the week, but most importantly the competition features some of the best talent in the Alps and from across the world.

The event's careful planning stretches as far as making it seem as if it's not really planned at all, and the organisers just fell out of bed and found themselves at the Grands Montets with some snowboards and a sound system. But one way or another it all comes together - and if you've ever wanted to see for real what you see on the extreme sports channel, this is where to do it.

when - usually early March, after the school half-terms have finished and when the weather is likely to be sunny and warmish. So many people come to watch or to compete or to go to the parties that you won't be able to escape the crowds no matter what you do - the resort is busy from first thing every morning to well into the small hours of the following day.

where - all the events take place on the Grands Montets, in the Snowpark next to the Lognan mid-station. You can walk to it from the cable car, so if you're just going to watch you needn't take your skis, though the rest of the mountain is still open for play as usual. The heats usually start around lunchtime, and with various breaks the competition bumbles along until around 4pm.

what - the Grands Montets park, which is ignored for much of the season, is properly designed and groomed for the ChamJam. It features a boarderX course, a big-air jump, a half-pipe, quarter-pipe, an assortment of precarious-looking rails, and a mogul run. The competition is divided into six separate events, one per day from Monday to Saturday.
boarderX - 4 boarders racing head-to-head down a course of rollers and banked turns. First to the end wins.
skierX - as boarderX but with skiers.
bosses des bosses - an inter-resort race down the mogul run (which has a jump at the end). Marks for speed

and style. Skiers only.
half-pipe - a style contest in the pipe (effectively a U-shaped chute), marked on execution and difficulty.
slopestyle - skiers and boarders using everything in the park to show of their skills. Marks for style and difficulty.
big air - as it sounds: skiers and boarders jumping to show off their best tricks. Always a favourite, for the crashes as much as for the amazing skills on display.

who can enter - anyone. You can, if you feel like it. For a decent chunk of Euros, you get to embarrass and/or hurt yourself alongside some extremely talented skiers and boarders. The ChamJam is appropriately tagged as a Pro-Am event, and though the competition is dominated by professionals, a lot of very able pseudo-sponsored and not-at-all sponsored seasonnaires enter too. But make no mistake - the standard is very high.

parties - if they can convince the local authorities, the organisers put up a marquee in town and from Wednesday to Saturday there is live music and DJing into the small hours. Ash and others of a similar ilk have played the ChamJam - and the marquee ticket is not extravagantly expensive. If the marquee doesn't make it, the same entertainment will relocate to a different venue, more than likely the Arbate in Cham Sud.

extreme contest

This is a 'watch-only' event, which takes place around the mid-season mark. The cream of the world's free-skiers show off their skills on a steep and rocky off-piste course. They are marked on speed, style, and difficulty of line - and the ability of the competitors has to be seen to be believed. The viewing point is the finish post, where the sponsors set up a food stall, and it makes a perfect place for a lazy lunch in the sunshine. Location is normally the Brévent - but look out for posters around town to confirm the details.

winter ride

A weekly freeride contest open to skiers and boarders, usually on the lower section of the Flégère (the location will be on posters around town and at the lift stations). The contest is a time-trial over an off-piste course marked solely by start and finish points. The event is as much social as it is competitive, and the majority of entrants are locals and seasonnaires. Like the ChamJam it's another loud music and experimental hairstyles occasion, and typical to the seasonnaire community the atmosphere is young, vibrant, and carefree.

world cup downhill

The Chamonix leg of the World Cup downhill takes place on the Kandahar run at Les Houches, a short drive down the valley from Chamonix. The event is usually in early January - information on the exact time is readily available on the internet and in ski magazines. Les Houches is not covered by the ChamSki pass, so you'll have to buy a separate day-pass to watch from the mountainside, but it will be well worth the money - seeing racers shoot past you at Ski Sunday speeds is something not to be missed.

24-hour ice race

Across the road from the Aiguille du Midi cable car is an ice-racing track, which for one weekend in late January or early February brings a rather different type of crowd to town. Ice racing is a cross between rallying and touring car racing, and though the event is a noisy affair which has nothing whatsoever to do with skiing, it is quite a spectacle. The drivers are world class, and a number of famous names have competed, including Nigel Mansell.

other events

There are various smaller events during the season, organized by the ESF or by local sponsors. Les Planards plays host to a number of evening displays under floodlights, including a big air display towards the end of the season. Events like these will be advertised on flyers and posters around town.

snow activities

If you feel you need a break from the downhill grind, there are plenty of other things to keep you entertained on the snow.

cross-country skiing

Ski de Fond has a special place in Chamonix life - many locals who are not so excited about the hordes of high-speed skiers on the pistes enjoy the snow in the relative quiet of the valley floor's extensive network of cross-country pistes, which are open 9am-5pm every day of the season. Chamonix and Argentière have a number of circuits, and throughout the winter the golf course in Les Praz functions as a multi-activity area. The valley has a total of about 70km of pistes.

heliskiing

Though illegal in France, you can make drops in neighbouring Italy or more expensively in Switzerland. Any of the guiding companies will organize trips for you, and as with on the Vallée Blanche, the cost of the trip will cover everything you need, including provision of avalanche transceivers.

huskies

If you've ever fancied being pulled along by a train of dogs, you can try it in Chamonix - either for 20 or 30 minutes as a passenger or on an hour-long instruction course at the end of which you should be able to control the sled on your own. Surprisingly, it is not so much exciting as relaxing, as the sled doesn't exactly reach break-neck speeds. Evolution 2 offer the husky experience, as do Husky Dalen, a husband and wife team who operate next to the leaners' slopes at La Vormaine.

night-skiing

On Thursday nights, Les Houches (see **other resorts**) opens the floodlit lower section of one of its pistes for free night-skiing. It is basically a promotional venture to raise the profile of the resort - but there's vin chaud on offer, and even skiing a gentle slope is a pretty different experience under lights.

snowshoeing

The spread out lift systems mean that there is an enormous area available for snowshoeing. All the guiding companies apart from Ski Sensations offer snowshoe trips - most popularly on the Mer de Glace, though with a guide you can go pretty much anywhere you want.

aiguille du midi

Chamonix's main non-skiing attraction, the Aiguille du Midi stands at 3842m, and on a clear day commands extraordinary views of the valley and the Alps beyond, along with the more immediate spectacle of seeing skiers hike down the arête that is the start of the Vallée Blanche. From the viewing platforms you may well be able to see extreme skiers heading down in various other directions, or mountaineers and climbers heading up the surrounding slopes and peaks.The construction itself is incredible, and the cable car ride alone will get your pulse racing... and the air is thin enough at the top to make you short of breath just from walking up stairs.

Temperatures on the Aiguille can be as low as -30°C, though on a sunny day in late season you will probably want to be in a t-shirt. The best approach is to take a number of layers. The cable car ride is expensive, but the trip is unforgettable. If you are not going to ski, you are better off going at lunchtime or later, when there will be no queue. See the **directory**.

mer de glace

The Montenvers train (**town e1**) takes you up to the Mer de Glace, the finish point for those skiing the Vallée Blanche. There is an ice grotto carved out of the glacier, which contains some rather incongruous ice sculptures and displays, but the trip is made worthwhile far more by the scenery. The 'attractions' are enough to keep young children entertained, but it all reeks of tourism and if you want a trip with a view (and can face the cable car) the Aiguille du Midi is a far more impressive experience.

le brévent

lift	time	information
planpraz gondola (6)	10m40s	**queues** common, fast-moving, up to 30 mins
altitude 2000 |2|	2m50s	**pistes** see la parsa **queues** occasional, morning, see below
brevent cable car 60	3m30s	**pistes** steep, wide, icy early morning, flat light by mid-afternoon **bumps** short, very steep **off-piste** steep, couloirs
la stade (1)	4m50s	**pistes** as la parsa **queues** very rare **other** often closed, see below
la parsa |4|	7m20s	**pistes** wide, gentle **bumps** none **off-piste** short, limited **queues** very common, afternoon, slow-moving
le cornu |3|	9m20s	**pistes** steep, wide, slushy in late season **bumps** short & long **off-piste** varied, bowls, couloirs **queues** common
la source |4|	3m10s	**pistes** short, track, see la charlanon **bumps** none **off-piste** trees **queues** very rare **other** flégère access
la charlanon |4|	3m40s	**pistes** short **bumps** short **off-piste** limited **queues** rare **other** return lift from flégère
flégère liaision 40	2m45s	**queues** rare **other** return lift from flégère
		queues occasional **other** see below

1 altitude 2000
2 la bergerie
3 le panoramic
X suggested picnic spot

altitude 2000 - when there is a long queue, a short hike past the bergerie restaurant takes you to the main piste down to la parsa, joining just below the beginner's slope. To avoid the queue at la parsa at the end of the day, take the stade drag, accessed by a traverse from the bottom of the cornu red run. It is sometimes closed and it's a téléski difficile, but it can save a lot of time. The quickest route to the flégère is via la source. In high winds the flégère's valley floor access is often closed.

key on inside back cover

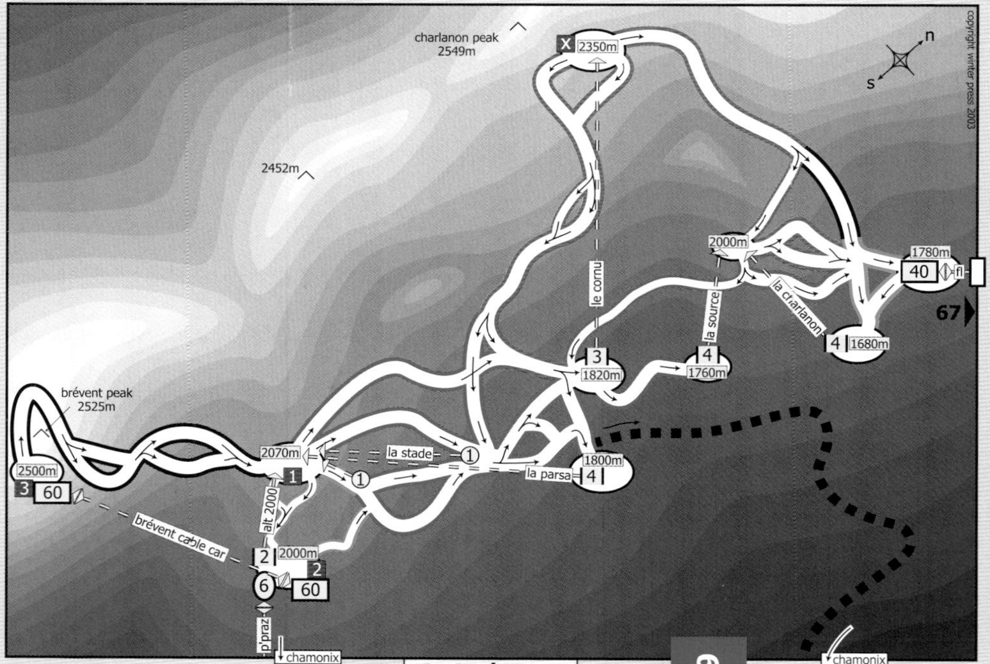

le brévent

la flégère

lift	time	information
flégère cable car 60	5m30s	**pistes** as la trappe, les evettes **queues** occasional, slow-moving **other** closes in high winds
la trappe |4|	6m25s	**pistes** gentle, wide **bumps** short, steep **off-piste** limited **queues** occasional **other** lift slow and often stopped
la chavanne |3|	5m20s	**pistes** gentle **bumps** none **off-piste** moderate, open **queues** rare **other** first lift to close at the end of the season
les evettes |3|	4m20s	**pistes** track, as la trappe **bumps** short **off-piste** trees **queues** rare
brévent liaison 40	2m45s	**other** brévent access
l'index |3|	6m55s	**pistes** varied, steep, sustained **bumps** extensive, steep **off-piste** moderate, open **queues** common
la floria ①	3m00s	**pistes** long, steep **bumps** none **off-piste** extensive, open **queues** very rare **other** runs sheltered in windy conditions

1 la chavanne
X suggested picnic spot

key on inside back cover

key on inside back cover

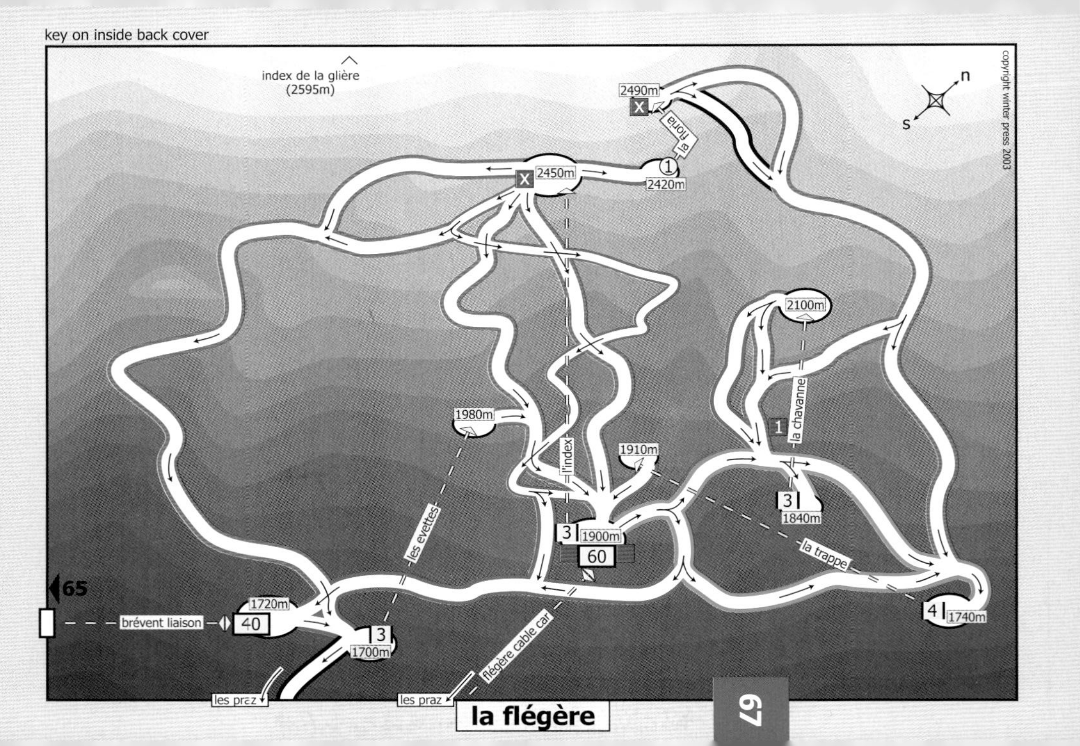

la flégère

les grands montets

lift	time	information
lognan 80	5m00s	**queues** very common, approx. 30 mins
plan joran |4|	11m10s	**other** see below
grands montets 60	7m00s	**pistes** none **bumps** long, steep, sustained **off-piste** long, steep, sustained, crevassed **queues** very common **other** see below
les marmottes |2|	8m00s	**pistes** short, gentle **bumps** short, gentle **off-piste** limited **queues** occasional
le bochard (10)	7m55s	**pistes** long, varied **bumps** long, steep **off-piste** varied, open **queues** common
la herse |2|	10m30s	**pistes** narrow **bumps** long, steep **off-piste** extensive, steep, open **queues** occasional **other** see below
la tabé |4|	6m10s	**pistes** short **bumps** none **off-piste** limited **queues** rare **other** snowpark access
plan roujon |4|	6m40s	**pistes** short, as la tabé and retour pendant **bumps** varied **off-piste** moderate, open **queues** rare
retour pendant |4|	8m20s	**pistes** narrow **bumps** varied **off-piste** moderate, trees **queues** occasional

1 lognan
2 plan joran
3 chalet refuge de lognan
4 snack bar 3300
5 la crèmerie du glacier
X suggested picnic spot

The plan joran chair is an alternative route up the mountain. It is long and cold, but the queue at the bottom will be shorter. You can also use this lift to come down. To use the grands montets cable car you need a ticket, available from the kiosk at the mid-station. Both the cable car and la herse are the ways to get to the chalet refuge de lognan.

key on inside back cover

key on inside back cover

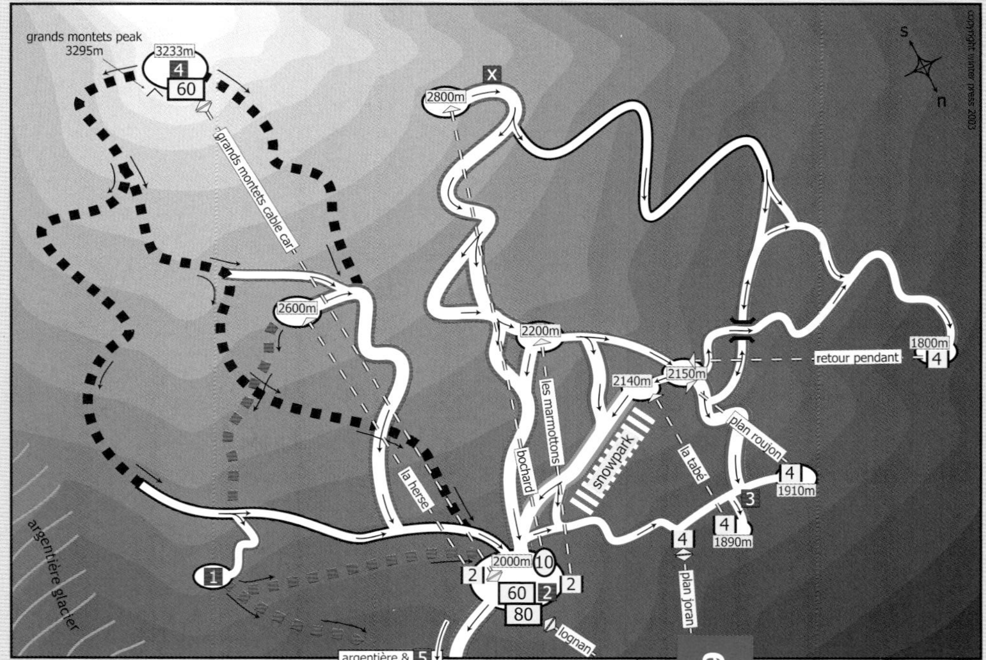

argentière & 5

les grands montets

le tour

lift	time	information
charamillon gondola (6)	8m20s	**queues** occasional
les autannes |4|	7m00s	**pistes** wide, gentle **bumps** none **off-piste** moderate, open **queues** common **other** can be very cold when windy
l'arve ①	4m10s	**pistes** as les autannes **queues** rare
col de balme ①	4m40s	**pistes** as les autannes **queues** rare **other** see below
l'aiguilette ①	3m50s	**pistes** varied **bumps** none **off-piste** see below **queues** rare
plan des reines ①	6m15s	**pistes** varied **bumps** none **off-piste** moderate, open **queues** occasional **other** long, awkward lift journey
tête de balme |4|	7m40s	**pistes** long **bumps** none **off-piste** extensive, trees **queues** occasional

1 chalet de charamillon
2 col de balme refuge hut
3 the snack-stop
X suggested picnic spot

The col de balme draglift is an alternative route to the col de balme refuge hut. It takes you closer than les autannes but the final walk is uphill. l'aiguillette leads to the start of a number of itinerary routes.

key on inside back cover

key on inside back cover

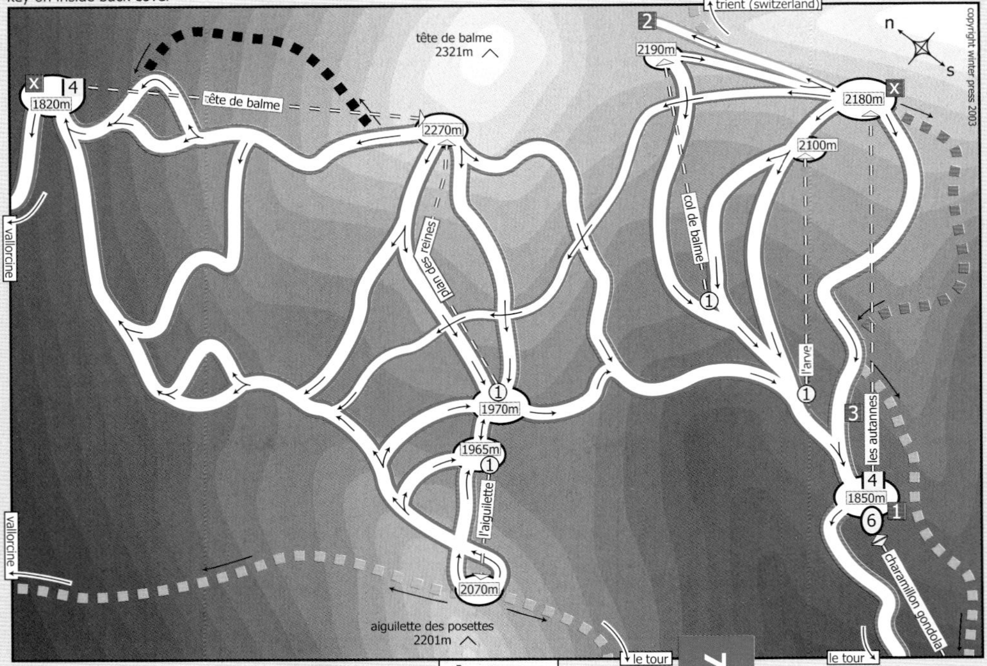

le tour

tête de balme 2321m
aiguilette des posettes 2201m
1820m
2270m
2190m
2180m
2100m
1970m
1965m
2070m
1850m
tête de balme
plan des reines
col de balme
l'arve
l'aiguilette
les autannes
charamillon gondola
trient (switzerland)
vallorcine
vallorcine
le tour
le tour
n
s

the resort

food & drink

Nowhere is the variety on offer in Chamonix more evident than in its choice of eateries. There are more than fifty restaurants, along with countless cafés, take-aways, boulangeries, pâtisseries...

restaurants

There are numerous different incarnations of restaurants in the modern European style, a huge selection of traditional Savoyarde places serving steaks, fondues and raclette, and also Italian, Chinese, Japanese, Indian, Mexican... there is even a MacDonalds.

In fact there is a gross overpopulation of Savoyarde restaurants. Most are much the same as each other, offering similar menus and similar service in similarly touristy 'traditional' surroundings. None are particularly bad, but some stand out as being particularly good. The reviews below are not intended to be comprehensive - rather they cover the best of what is on offer.

useful information

opening hours - most restaurants close on one evening during the week, usually Monday or Tuesday. Wednesday is traditionally the chalet staff night off, and so is the busiest night of the week for restaurants, so it is a good idea to book well in advance.

snapshot

for something...

- at breakfast - atelier café
- cheap - eldorado
- cheesy - crèmerie paccard
- reassuringly expensive - le chaudron
- reassuringly good - munchie
- late - belouga
- meaty - le carlina
- romantic - l'atmosphère
- by the river - grand central

sittings - some restaurants operate on a two-sitting basis, with the first sitting around 7 or 7:30pm, and the second around 9 or 9:30pm. They are usually quite relaxed about arriving late or overstaying the first sitting, but in many places you won't be able to book a table for 8pm.

prices

The featured restaurants are differentiated by the grading (1)-(5) reflecting the approximate price per head for a main course excluding drinks. The number is not an indication of quality - all of the reviewed restaurants are in our opinion of good quality. The price ranges are as follows:

(1) under €8
(2) €8-14
(3) €15-22
(4) €23-30
(5) over €30

All featured restaurants accept most major credit cards.

le carlina (4)

map - town e3
t 0450 53 18 98
open 11am-11pm
food traditional savoyarde
bar ✓

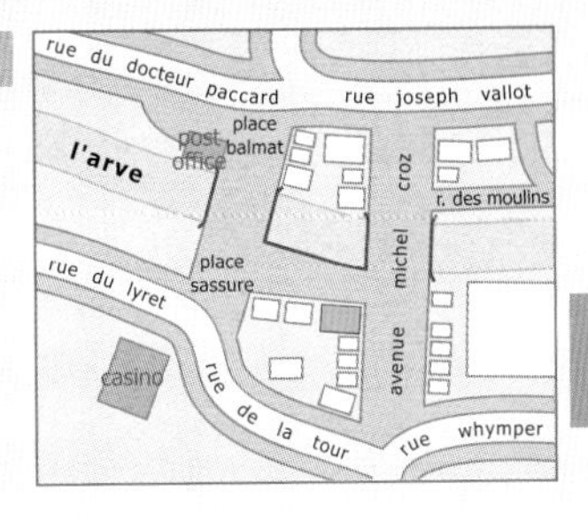

A superbly friendly place right in the centre of town. Le Carlina has a huge menu of steaks and fondues which are all deliciously well prepared, and served with expert off-hand professionalism. The restaurant is in quite a large open plan area and does not look like a traditional local restaurant - but if you want an authentically French experience then you are better off here than in some of the other local Savoyarde restaurants that spend more effort keeping up appearances.

Unusually, they do not take reservations so you will always be able to get a table, and normally with no more than a 5 or 10 minute wait - though if you are coming with a large group it is worth calling ahead to warn them. If you do end up sitting at the bar for a bit, you can drink your pre-dinner beers out of litre-sized glasses, which are big enough to make you light-headed simply by looking at them.

Le Carlina is also open all day, so if you're taking a day away from the slopes you can indulge yourself in a big lunch, or while away your lazy afternoon snacking or sipping coffee on the large riverside terrace.

« local »

le chaudron (5)

map - town f3
t 0450 53 40 34
open 6pm-11pm
food traditional savoyarde
bar ×

As expensive as it is small, the Cauldron squeezes traditional Savoyarde excellence into minute surroundings. It is a family run restaurant in the centre of the Rue des Moulins offering the range of fondues and steaks you will find everywhere else, but presented with a much more personal and intimate touch. This is not a place to go to in a large group, but if you want good food, cosy surroundings, friendly attentiveness - and if you don't mind paying for your cheese - Le Chaudron is one of the best choices in town.

la crèmerie paccard (3)

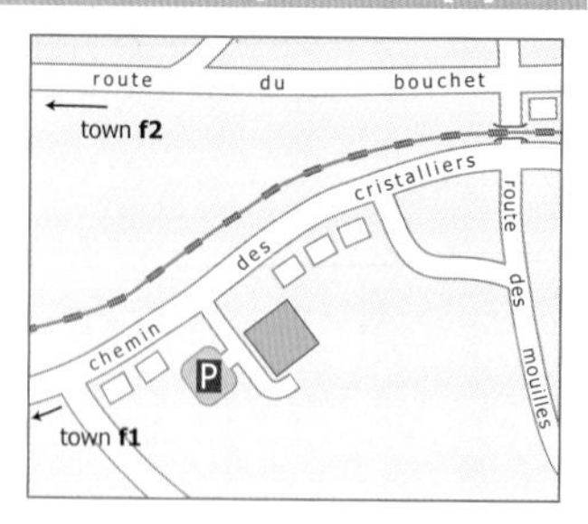

map - valley c2
t 0450 53 13 87
open 7:30pm-11pm
food traditional savoyarde
bar ✓

A lovely and authentic restaurant attached to the Hermitage Paccard (see **hotels**). It is a large place with a very different décor and feel to most restaurants: every detail has been carefully considered and the atmosphere created is friendly and welcoming. The food is equally well presented with a wide range of restaurant specialities - the *tartiflette des Aravis* is especially recommended, as are the local ice creams for dessert. It is a 5 minute walk from the centre of town and so is not ideally convenient - though it is close to the MBC (see **bars**).

gecko (2)

map - town f/g4
t 0450 53
open 9am-11pm
food traditional savoyarde
bar ✓

As much a bar as it is a restaurant, and about as casual as they come. Open all day and quieter all day than most places thanks to its being a short distance from the centre. The menu is mostly steak and fondue, all very reasonably priced and all as tasty as you will find anywhere else - and with a vegetarian option. Gecko has very welcoming French ownership, a *très petite* terrace, and small TVs (which show mostly Eurosport, so don't go hoping for English football).

l'impossible (4)

map - town a4
t 0450 53 20 36
open 7pm-11pm
food traditional savoyarde
bar ×

By reputation one of the best Savoyarde restaurants in Chamonix. A large converted farm house on the outskirts of Chamonix Sud, which creates a warm cosy feel in spite of its size. There is a sense here that the staff take pride in their food and service that is missing in some of the more central Savoyarde restaurants. The menu is a comprehensive range of everything you would expect to find with many specialities, and the food is every bit as good as it sounds. Its only drawback is that is not in the centre of town - but it is right next to the Jekyll (see **bars**) and there is parking across the road.

le pitz (2)

map - town e/f2
t 0450 53 05 08
open 12pm-11pm
food traditional savoyarde, pizzas
bar ×

Unfortunately named, le Pitz is in fact a very friendly and welcoming pizzeria that also serves all the Savoyarde specialities along with a variety of crêpes and other sweet things. It is open from lunchtime onwards, and has a bar and a large heated terrace where you can sip your vin chaud. The roadside setting isn't quite as charming as the pedestrianised town centre, but if you need something as soon as you get off the bus, or if you feel like going somewhere a little bit away from the crowds on the main drag, le Pitz could be your place.

snapshot

in tartiflette we trust...
Chamonix is nestled in the Haute Savoy, a region with a strong tradition for local cuisine. Though you can find pretty much any kind of food in the valley, more than half of the restaurants specialise in the regional dishes of fondue (meat or cheese), raclette (a dish made purely from melted cheese, normally served with potatoes) and tartiflette (layers of potatoes mixed with cheese and crème fraîche, cooked in a massive wok-style pan).

Savoyarde food is a long way removed from the French chic of nouvelle cuisine - the portions are large, and there's no fitting them into a low-carbohydrate diet. Fortunately, the high altitude and low temperatures of the mountains mean that your body burns a lot more fat than usual - so rather than making you put on weight, the stodginess of the food is what will keep your muscles going through six days of hard skiing.

« general »

l'atmosphère (4)

map - town e3
t 0450 55 97 97
open 7pm-11pm
food french
bar ✓

One of the best restaurants, Atmosphère has impeccable service and a lovely interior with some seating overlooking the river. Centrally located and with an excellent range of choices on the menu, including some outstanding fish dishes (specialities include lobster, grilled seabass fillet and a superb tuna carpaccio). The restaurant is French run and feels slightly formal, but is very welcoming with it. Like many restaurants in Chamonix, Atmosphère runs two-sittings, the first at around 7:15pm and the second around 9:15pm - though in practice they aren't too officious about the timing. Because of its location it tends to be very busy, so it is well worth booking.

bumble bee (3)

map - town f3
t 0450 53 50 03
open 7pm-11pm
food greek, spanish, tapas
bar ✓

A very cosy and informal restaurant at the top of the Rue des Moulins. Bumble Bee is a small English run place and offers a genuinely personal family welcome - if what you want is somewhere you can chat to the owners as you eat, this is it. The menu is not as extensive as some larger restaurants but the food is well chosen and expertly prepared, and you will be full when you leave. Tables get booked up quickly, especially for the early evening - and while it's not a big enough place to sit at the bar and wait for a table, given its location you won't be short of alternatives for a pre-dinner drink or two.

eden (5)

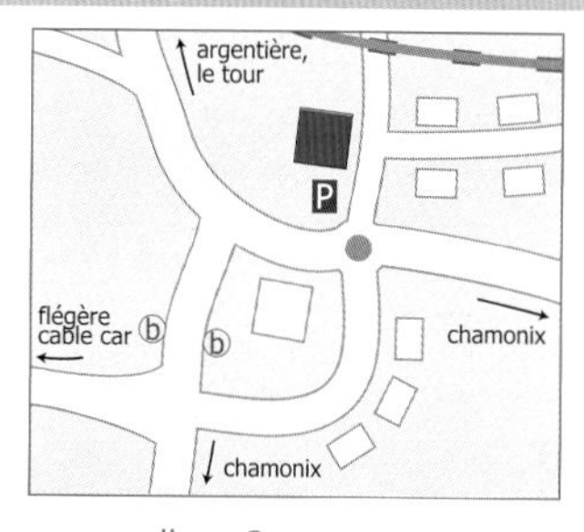

map - valley c3
t 0450 53 18 43
open 7pm-11pm
food french
bar ✓

Quite possibly the best restaurant in the valley - at the Eden hotel in Les Praz. Set menus range from the very affordable to the *menu degustation* at around €80, and all dishes are available à la carte. The beef carpaccio, veal fillet and crème brulee are especially recommended, but all dishes are sumptuously tasty, flawlessly prepared and presented by a chef with a real enthusiasm for his food. The restaurant is smartish, but with no obligation to formality, and the service is infallible in both the restaurant and the adjoining bar, which stays open until the last customer leaves.

eldorado (1)

map - town c4
t 0450 53 31 23
open 11am-11pm
food tex-mex
bar ✓

A very informal restaurant on the outskirts of the centre. Eldorado is only a 5 minute walk from most pubs and is equally accessible from the centre and from Cham Sud. The food is typical tex-mex, tasty and filling, but the main attraction of Eldorado is the relaxed atmosphere. It is an excellent place for a large party or a family, as it has none of the pretensions of grander restaurants and the prices are low enough that the bill won't put you off your lunch the next day. It also has a long bar to slide your tequila glass down, five internet stations, and serves omelettes at lunchtime.

munchie (3)

map - town f3
t 0450 53 45 41
open 6pm-11pm
food french
bar ✓

The best restaurant on the Rue des Moulins, serving first class food at reasonable prices. The menus and the presentation are as you would expect to find in a good London restaurant, and there is something for all tastes - and some wonderful desserts for those with a sweet tooth. The service is intelligent and friendly, and its location makes it an ideal place for those with pre- or post-dinner plans. It is on three levels: two small eating areas separated by a little bar on the middle floor which tends to be a seasonnaire hangout. The staff are mostly Scandinavian and so speak perfect English. As ever, book in advance as Munchie is very popular.

« and the rest »

annapurna (3)

map - town c4
t 0450 55 81 39
open 6pm-11pm
food indian
bar ×

In case you're missing your chicken madras, Annapurna offers a quality way to satisfy your needs. It is comparable to the more upmarket Indians in England, so don't go hoping for a festival of lager and vindaloo.

le dragon d'or (2)

map - town c3
t 0450 53 37 25
open 6pm-11pm
food chinese
bar ✓

Chamonix's Chinese, on the main drag in Cham Sud. Sweet & sour pork is surprisingly satisfying on a skiing holiday - you can lap up those calorific sauces safe in the knowledge that it's all going to get burned off in the snow.

satsuki (2)

map - town f/g4
t 0450 53 21 99
open 12pm-2:30pm, 6pm-11pm
food japanese
bar ×

Just out of the centre, Satsuki is a small and simple restaurant that opens for lunch and dinner with a broad menu of Japanese specialities, a very enthusiastic owner, and very reasonably priced sushi to eat in or take-away.

la spiga d'oro (3)

map - town c4
t 0450 53 06 49
open 6pm-11pm
food italian
bar ×

A combined shop and restaurant which displays an exotic array of Italian ingredients, which you can buy from the ground floor counter, or eat at a table upstairs. Proximity to the Italian border means the food is all fresh and authentic.

le tetras (2)

map - town b/c3
t 0450 53 33 97
open 6pm-11pm
food tex-mex, pizza, savoyarde
bar ✓

Standard fare tex-mex in the heart of Cham Sud, with a cheerful approach and a bustling atmosphere. Few surprises on the menu, but no complaints and if you're staying in the southern *quartier* this is good food without the walk.

macdonalds (1)

map - town e3
t 0450 53 31 13
open 8am-11pm
food burgers
bar ×

A high-ceilinged restaurant at the end of the Avenue Michel Croz, MacDonald's sells a none-too-healthy range of burgers and chips, chicken and dips, and a variety of breakfasts. The décor is an odd mix of plastic and wood, which is a little out of keeping with the usual ski-resort warmth - but though there is also a mass-produced feel to the food, it is curiously appealing. There is a special menu for children, five internet stations (though no good coffee)... MacDonald's is open all day and does not take reservations - you will rarely have to wait for a table, and the service though often surly is probably the fastest of anywhere in town.

restaurants

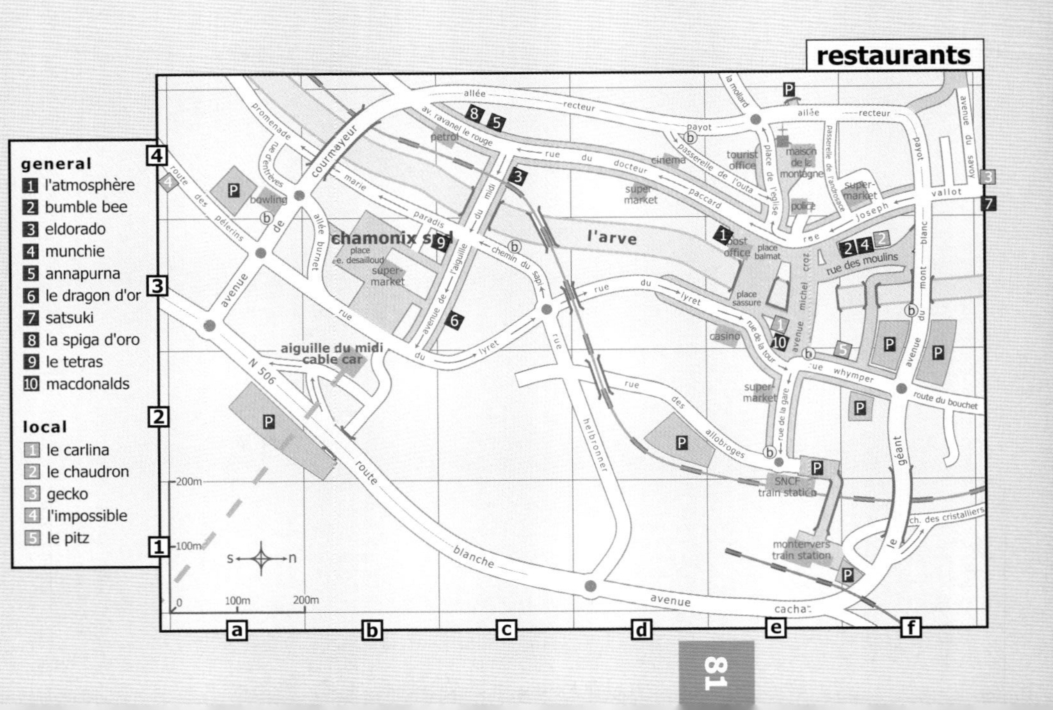

cafés

If the après in the bars is a little too hectic, or you need a quick recharge before you head into it, Chamonix has various businesses devoted to providing a slightly more relaxing way of life. There are numerous boulangeries and pâtisseries dotted around the town which give you plenty of opportunity to stock up on calories, but if you are if are looking for something a little different, your options range from coffee and bagels to cheese and fine wines.

Most of Chamonix's cafés are open through the lunchtime siesta, so if you find your shopping trip abruptly cut short at midday when the shops close, they give you somewhere to while away the 2 hour break.

l'atelier café (2)

map - town e3
t 0450 53 32 36
open 8:30am-7pm
food cooked breakfast & pm snacks
terrace ✓

A good spot for a bacon and egg breakfast, or for Chamonix's best *croque monsieur* in the afternoon. The Atelier is right in the centre of town, by the river, and the large terrace makes it a perfect spot in good weather. When it's cold outside, the high-ceilinged interior is a warm and welcoming place to round off a day on the slopes without losing your personal space to a horde of beer swilling karaoke experts.

le bistro des sports (1)

map - town f3
t 0450 53 00 46
open 8:30am-11pm
food bar food
terrace ×

On Chamonix's busy main street, and generally very French... certainly very local, but entirely welcoming to anyone wanting an espresso and a seat away from the crowds. The Bistro opens early, stays open until the evening, and has a bar in case you need some alcohol to wash down your coffee. The name is misleading though - don't go here if you're looking for big TV screens to watch the football, because there aren't any.

la crêperie brettone (1)

map - town c3
t 0450 53 16 04
open 11:45am-9:30pm
food crêpes
terrace ×

Although their tag-line of being 'the only crêperie in Chamonix' isn't quite true (there's one by the hotel Vallée Blanche on the Rue du Lyret), the Crêperie Bretonne is the pick of the two. The menu offers a staggering number of *galettes* (savoury pancakes) with questionable fillings like chicken curry, or sausages and mustard, and a more comfortable

grand central (1)

map - town f3
t 0450 53 56 09
open 8am-8pm
food bagels & coffee
terrace ✓

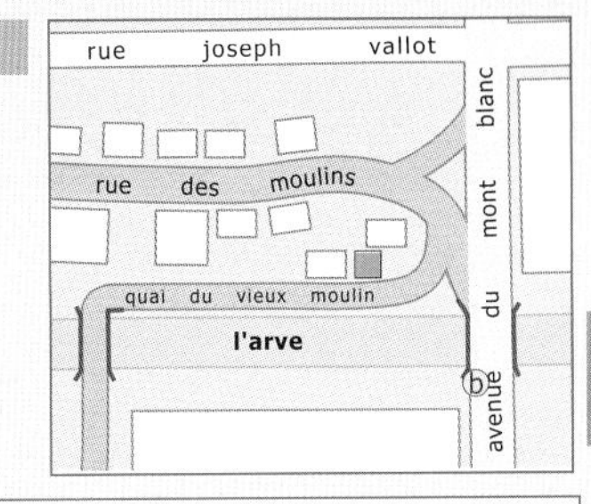

The only place in town where you can get your latté fix. Unless you like your coffee compressed into a shot mug, Chamonix can be quite frustrating - but Grand Central offers a comprehensive coffee menu alongside a creative list of smoothies and health drinks, and bagels imported from New York and stuffed to the brim with an original and mouth-watering range of fillings.

The interior isn't quite big enough to fit a sofa - this is the coffee shop experience, Chamonix style: down by the river on the edge of the Rue des Moulins, it is the perfect place for an outdoor breakfast under the gaze of Mont Blanc, for a take-away coffee on your way to the Alpina bus stop, or for an afternoon beer and snack on your way into town. Grand Central has a late licence, and from time to time will stay open beyond the advertised 8pm closing time, but whenever you go you will find an individual, personal, and genuinely friendly welcome.

Along with offering food to take-away you can also pre-book a packed lunch to take with you up the mountain - just drop in or telephone the day before, and your bagel will be ready wrapped for you as you head off to the slopes in the morning.

range of crêpes (the sweet version) which you'll probably be more inclined to indulge in. The interior feels a little plasticky, but it's a good place to fill up your stomach - and indeed serves a very good *tartiflette* on the set menu.

gouthé (1)

map - town f3
t 0450 53 58 95
open 4pm-7pm
food pâtisserie
terrace ×

On the Rue des Moulins opposite the Bureau des Guides, Gouthé boasts what is possibly the most enticing window display in town. It is a pâtisserie like no other, with a fabulous range of homemade cakes and pastries and a drinks menu which offers - amongst other things - four different types of hot chocolate. If you have a weakness for sweet things, Gouthé is one place where you can consume enough calories to keep you skiing for months.

le lapin agile (2)

map - town e2/3
t -
open 11am-11pm
food assiettes of meat & cheese
terrace ✓ (small)

The Agile Rabbit is a wine bar - one of only two in Chamonix - with a vast array of fine wines from around the world. Most can be bought by the glass, and the owner will be only too happy to discuss their origins with the discerning drinker - if your French is up to it. To balance your palette, the menu also offers a selection of meats and cheeses and the three small and private rooms are also available for dinner. All in all the Lapin is a refined and very different experience, in a town that at times can feel a little too touristy or a little too local.

la potinière (2)

map - town e4
t 0450 53 02 84
open 10am-11pm
food classic french bistro
terrace ✓

Better known as 'the Pot', this central eatery is more restaurant than café, and has a full menu which runs through to the evening. In addition to main courses they serve a selection of salads and a wonderful stringy-cheese French onion soup, and the busy terrace and good-humoured service make it a favourite lunchtime spot when the weather starts to warm up.

late night & take-away

Despite the huge range of restaurants in town, there are any number of reasons to want take-away food. If you fancy eating standing up, or if all the restaurants closed before you got to them, you have plenty of choices for a quick bite. Surprisingly, nothing stays open after 2am, but until then the centre of town does a bustling trade in burgers and baguettes. Options in Cham Sud are a little more limited, but wherever you are you're not too far from somewhere that sells hot food late at night.

au four à bois (2)

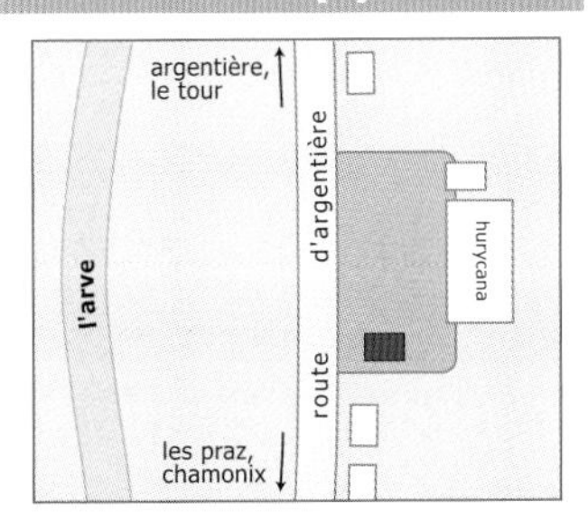

map - valley c5
t 0681 05 51 81
open 6pm-late
food pizza

If you have transport this is quite the best way to eat pizza - call ahead and order or simply drive to the parking outside Hurycana sports and see your meal flame-baked in front of you. Given that it only offers pizza, the menu is pretty imaginative and none of the toppings are added until you order. Even the bases are exquisitely tasty. In the evening, with no traffic, Au Four à Bois is only 2 minutes from Argentière and 10 minutes from Chamonix, and is well worth the journey.

belouga (1)

map - town c4
t -
open 12pm-2am
food hot sandwiches

The best take-away place in Chamonix. A very wide range of delicious and surprisingly healthy toasted sandwiches, which come with 'steak' (burger) as an additional option, but which are mostly a blend of meats, cheeses and vegetables that feels rather like a Pizza Express menu. Options include Camembert, goats cheese, lamb, jambon cru... you can buy beer should you want to drink on the street, and about halfway through the season when the weather warms up they sell ice creams. Nothing is missing - even the chips are excellent and there is a range of ten or so sauces to go with your choice of food.

cappadoce (1)

map - town b3
t 0450 53 20 04
open 11am-2am
food kebabs

Chamonix's only kebab shop, though not quite what you might be used to. The Doner meat tastes more or less like meat, which is somehow not entirely satisfying, and the cardboardy pitta bread is rather different to what you get in England. The non-Doner menu is the normal range of chicken and burgers and while the food is uninspiring, if kebabs are your thing this is your only option.

fed up (1)

map - town f3
t -
open 4pm-11pm
food chish & fips

An authentic Scottish run fish & chip shop, opposite Bar d'Up on the Rue des Moulins. Fed Up as a policy does not sell burgers, but it does sell proper battered fish and chunky chips wrapped in English newspaper - if it weren't for the snow and mountains you could almost be by the sea in the rain. Also on the menu is the Stovie, a Scottish speciality blend of minced beef and onions, served in a baguette, which will warm you up on the coldest evenings.

the garage (1)

map - town b3
t 0450 53 64 69
open 10pm-4am
food baguettes

The Garage is a night club, of course, but since there is nowhere to go for food after 2pm, the cloakroom here is the last place where it is available - they stock a basket full of baguettes which they sell as you leave. Don't pass up the opportunity if it's 4am, because you won't find anywhere else open until the boulangeries get going at around 6am.

midnight express (1)

map - town e3
t -
open 12pm-2am
food crusty burgers

A popular take-away joint which specialises in big crusty buns filled with far more chips than burger. The menu is a typical variety of patties and cheeses and fillings and sauces, but something in the hectic ordering process often seems to get lost in the translation. Any attempts at French are likely to be met with an attempt at English... but if what you need is carbohydrate stodge, you can't go far wrong.

poco loco (1)

map - town d3/4
t 0450 53 43 03
open 12pm-2am
food less crusty burgers

Just along from Midnight Express, and somewhat better quality unless you like the 'crusty bread filled with chips' approach. Poco Loco sells baguettes and burgers, large helpings of chips, crêpes, and everything else you would expect... and also has extremely friendly ownership, a bar inside and an upstairs eating area - possibly the narrowest one in the world - which has a little TV and is a hangout for locals and some of the younger ESF instructors.

cafés & take away

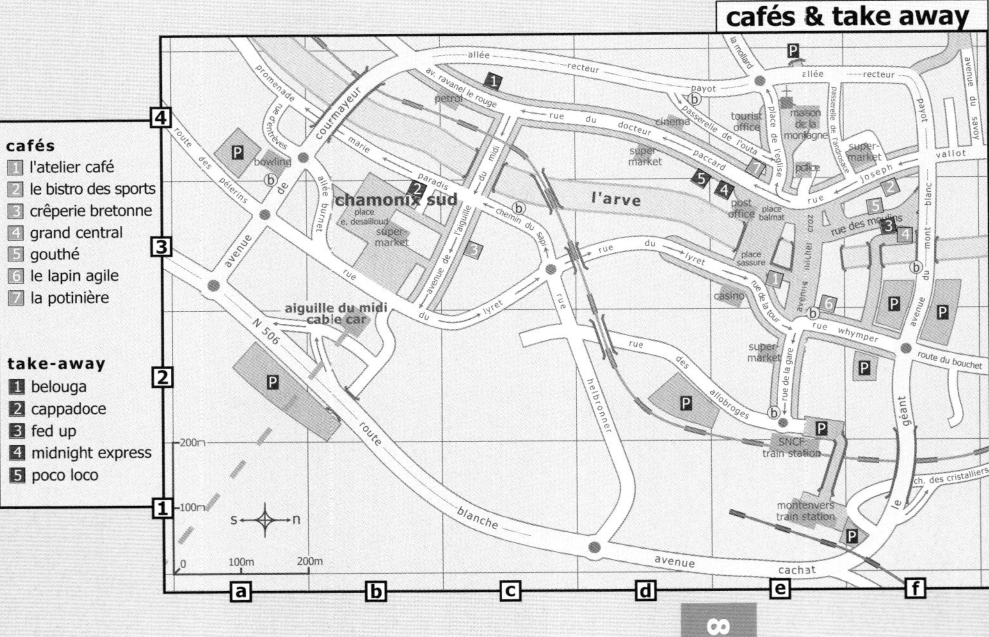

après-ski & nightlife

Chamonix has the most diverse and perhaps the liveliest après-ski in the Alps. This is basically thanks to the size of the place - it has more than 30 bars (not including hotel bars), the majority of which open at 4pm and stay open until 1 or 2 in the morning. Whatever your taste may be, with a bit of effort you will find something in Chamonix to keep you happy. Any men looking for holiday romance need to be careful - the valley has a reputation for having the highest male to female ratio in the Alps, and there certainly are some bars where you will be hard pushed to spot a girl in the throng of drinkers.

snapshot

après...
beer - mbc
cheer - wild wallabies
atmosphere - chambre neuf

après après...
english chill - cybar
french chic - l'expédition
swedish beauty - south bar

and dawn-breakers
party people - dicks t-bar
true clubbing - l'arbate
cosy cool - cantina

bars & pubs

The majority of the bars are run and staffed by ex-pats and seasonnaires from English speaking countries - and anyone working in a bar will be able to speak enough English to take your order. That's not to say that you shouldn't try to speak the language if you can, but the chances are that you'll be talking to someone who would understand you better in your native tongue.

useful information

social calendar - Chamonix is big enough that there isn't really a timetable to the week. Almost every night is busy somewhere - the only exception being Saturday evenings which thanks to being the first night of most people's holiday is rather unpredictable - arriving seems to inspire either mass hysteria or utter lethargy, and accordingly the pubs and clubs are either hugely busy or completely deserted. Wednesday is typically the chalet night off, but as fewer than half of Chamonix's seasonnaires work in chalets this is no reason to expect town to be significantly busier than usual.

prices

You should expect to pay €10ish for a pitcher of beer, though depending on your choice of establishment this can vary by a couple of Euros in either direction. Cocktails, 'pints' and wine come more or less at London prices, so while nothing is cheap you shouldn't get too much of a surprise when you get the bill.

« bars & pubs »

bar d'up

map - town f3
t 0450 53 91 33
open 5pm-2am
food ×
tv ✓
live music ✓

At the main-road end of the Rue des Moulins, Bar d'Up pulls off the 'loud music and lots of beer' approach common to many après bars. There is always something going on: regular live bands, late night themed events, Sky Sports for live rugby and football (on very small televisions), a pool table... it is most popular with the early 20s crowd, who are probably least put off by its low-ceilings and slightly boxy feel. It does not serve food, but the nominally linked Fed Up is just across the way (see **take-away**).

chambre neuf

map - town e2
t 0450 55 89 81
open 7am-2am
food 12pm-3pm
tv ✓ (very small)
live music ✓ (every day)

Perhaps the best (almost certainly the busiest) après bar in Chamonix. It is relatively small and not wonderfully designed, but the excellent live music between 5pm and 7pm packs the English and Scandinavian crowds in, and from then there is rarely a lull until it closes. If you want to escape the jam, the terrace is the perfect place to watch the mountains flare pink with the sunset. Along with the atmosphere and homely wooden décor, it is popular thanks to its location - attached to the hotel Gustavia, it is 2 minutes' walk from the Montenvers train, and the Chamonix Bus stops on the doorstep.

cybar

map - town f3
t 0450 53 69 70
open 10am-2am
food 3pm-9pm
tv ✓
live music ✓

The Cybar is in a lot of ways the heart of Chamonix bar culture. Its diverse attractions include a huge main area, regular events and live music, four levels (if you include the Bar des Moulins downstairs), 24 internet stations, a DVD lounge, sofas, a pool table and a large projection screen for live sport or extreme videos... you can also borrow games like Jenga, Scrabble and chess from behind the bar. The food is limited and uninspiring, but if you need to eat there are plenty of restaurants outside on the Rue des Moulins. If you need to dance, Dick's is only 20 yards away. The Cybar is a big part of the seasonnaire social scene, and the staff all speak English as a first language, so you needn't feel the pressure to bumble through in French.

l'expédition

map - town e3
t 0450 53 57 68
open 4pm-4am
food ×
tv ×
live music ✓

If Holly Golightly lived in Chamonix, this is where she would go to drink. Slightly more expensive than most other bars - but slightly classier too, without feeling at all pretentious. One of the few places you'll find flair bar staff, and one of only two bars that stays open until 4am. A smallish but well organised space, with comfortable seating and music that isn't all pop. It is another favourite with the locals, and is often busy to the end with those who want to avoid the mass market feel of the clubs. Situated neatly at the end of the Rue des Moulins, it is enough off the drunken track to avoid the crowds.

goophy

map - town e2
t 0450 55 33 42
open 4pm-2am
food ✓ (restaurant)
tv ×
live music ×

Opposite Chambre Neuf and often just as packed, though more of a night haunt than an après bar. It attracts a slightly younger, 'cooler' crowd, and is popular with seasonnaires and locals as well as holidaymakers. Most evenings there is a live DJ - the music is varied and can be a little unusual, but the atmosphere is busy, lively and loud at all times. Contrary to the Chamonix reputation there are often girls in Goophy's - though as likely as not they will have dreadlocks for hair and pro snowboarders for boyfriends. The back section has a good restaurant - but be aware that during the week of the ChamJam this is likely to be closed as the eating area is used as the centre of operations by the event organisers.

jekyll

map - town a4
t 0450 55 99 70
open 5pm-2am
food 7pm-11pm (restaurant)
tv ×
live music ✓

Cham Sud's Irish pub - which is dark, often very busy, and always very lively. The Jekyll has regular and rowdy live music and events, and along with a wide range of beers on tap sells litre jugs of cocktails. The Jekyll could just as well be described as a restaurant, as a decent food menu is available at any table and the room on the ground floor - which has a couple of long picnic tables in a space just about big enough to hold them - is an excellent place for a large group to eat and drink. The food is very good and the service attentive - be sure to book ahead.

mbc

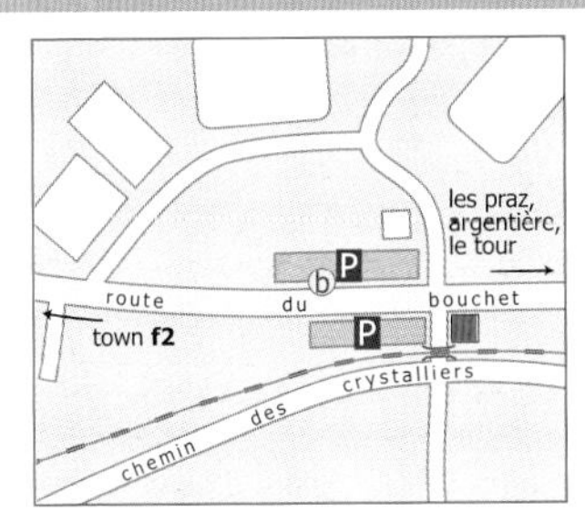

map - valley c2
t 0450 53 61 69
open 3:30pm-2am
food ✓
tv ×
live music ✓

The most welcoming of any of the bars in Chamonix. The only micro-brewery in the valley, with some excellent *pression* (draught) beers, generously portioned good quality food and bar snacks (including great nachos), beautiful wooden décor, and the 'camel' - which would be a giraffe anywhere else - a three litre tower of beer with its own tap which is brought your table so you can help yourself. The MBC is a 5 minute walk away from the town centre, so while it is often busy it is rarely filled with drunken hordes - the majority of the crowd is more 'mountain guide' than 'powder virgin'. It is Canadian run, has regular live music in the late aftenoon and occasionally a DJ in the evenings, and is very popular with locals and the more discerning of the seasonnaire population.

the pub

map - town d4
t 0450 55 92 88
open 4pm-2am
food ×
tv ✓
live music ✓

A friendly and busy little place which appeals as much to Chamonix's French contingent as to holiday-makers. It is not a 'cool' bar like many of the places in town - though it can sometimes feel a bit narrow and cramped, it is a fine place to spend an evening away from predictable après revelry. The Pub never gets too rowdy - when it is full it just feels very full. The music is an unpredictable mix of styles - though there is occasionally a live DJ, tunes are normally chosen from the CD collection behind the bar. Live bands at the Pub are rare and a little different to the norm - more likely to be jazz than loud guitars.

safari

map - town c4
t 0450 53 62 99
open 4pm-2am
food ×
tv ✓
live music ×

A dark and literally underground bar, which fits a lot into a little space. Odd décor gives it a slightly quirky feel, but it offers everything the larger bars have, just on a smaller scale: a pool table, an internet station, free Playstation 2, and a big TV screen that shows live rugby and football and extreme videos the rest of the time. Safari is also about the cheapest bar in town, and has its own DJ every night - or if you fancy moving on you can get to the Plaza nightclub without even having to go outside.

south bar

map - town b3
t 0450 55 43 07
open 7:30am-12pm, 4pm-1:30am
food ✓ (7:30am-11:30am)
tv ×
live music ✓

The centre of Cham Sud's social life. The South Bar is run by Swedes, staffed by Swedes and frequented by Swedes - and therefore also by English people looking to meet Swedes. The narrow upstairs gets very crowded after 11pm. Downstairs you'll probably find a little more space, though fewer seats, and the atmosphere is decidedly cosier and more clubby. Regular live bands, local DJs, theme nights (including topless barmen) and proximity to the Garage all contribute to the South Bar's popularity. The only drawback is the toilet - there is only one, which makes for yellow snow in the surrounding alleyways.

la terrasse

map - town e3
t 0450 53 09 95
open 4pm-2am
food ✓
tv ×
live music ✓

More expensive, and more up-market than some bars. It is very definitely split between its two levels - the downstairs is no different to anywhere else but the first floor has a more refined feel, and the live music and entertainment is more subdued than you would find in places like Chambre Neuf or Wallabies. That said, La Terasse has a DJ some nights, and later in the evening it can be just as rowdy as anywhere else.

wild wallabies

map - town e3
t 0450 53 01 31
open 4pm-2am
food ✓ restaurant
tv ✓
live music ×

A large open plan bar with a bit of everything: sofas, table football, pool, a small dance floor, a restaurant section... it is nothing out of the ordinary but while it lacks character it is lively and loud almost every night of the week. The age range in the bar is broader than in some places, and the restaurant is pleasant and quiet in spite of its proximity to the rest of the bar. The music is mostly current pop, and Wallabies is a stop on the package trip pub crawls, so don't be surprised to find a large drunken crowd there in the middle of the week.

nightclubs

All but two of Chamonix's bars close by 2am, and those not so keen on catching the first lift in the morning head to one of the town's nightclubs. Clubbing in Chamonix is much like in any other ski resort, except perhaps for the broader choice of dancefloors - wherever you are in town there is likely to be a club a short walk away.

useful information

dress code - aside from the Garage's curious no-hat policy, you will not encounter a dress code anywhere in Chamonix - you are as well off in your ski gear as your party frock, as least as far as the bouncers are concerned.

girls who like boys - as with any club in the world, helping out the boy-girl ratio won't do your queuing time any harm - crowds of females are pretty rare, and so are highly prized by door staff. When there's no queue, work on getting them to drop the cover charge.

prices

Cover charges vary from place to place, and also depending on what time you arrive, but apart from at the Arbate they're nothing that will trouble your wallet. Cloakrooms also levy a minimal fee - but clubs make their money from drinks prices, which are significantly higher than in the bars.

l'arbate

map - town c3
t 0450 53 44 43
open 5pm-4am
entrance weekends & theme nights

A ski-resort slice of Ibiza nightlife. In case your holiday isn't already costing you enough, you can lose your remaining Euros in Chamonix's only real club - the main weekly night hosts name DJs from across the European club scene, and the blend of skiing euphoria and properly mixed music makes for a wild and memorable experience. It's not for the half-hearted and it's not cheap, but if the weather's bad or you'd rather see the dawn than the rest of the day, the Arbate is your place.

la cantina

map - town f4
t 0450 53 83 80
open 5pm-2am
entrance free

A small and out of the way club that is one of the only places that you'll find music that isn't just repetitive commercial dance. La Cantina hosts regular guest DJs championing diverse musical styles - an assortment of reggae, hip-hop, drum and bass, and chill out nights. The best way to find out what's on is to look for the posters around town. There's not much space that isn't dancefloor, but La Cantina regulars are generally more interested in the music than in checking their make-up (or other people's).

dick's t-bar

map - town f3
t 0450 53 19 10
open 10pm-4am
entrance free before 1am, cheap thereafter

The Chamonix branch of Dick's T-Bars, made famous by the original in Val d'Isere. A standard fare club with two levels and a slightly cramped dancefloor. Nightclub prices too - everything a little more expensive than in the bars - but for that you get the more outgoing of the English tourist and seasonnaire population. There are regular guest DJs, occasional theme nights, and the music is generally what you would expect in any commercial club in England - a bit of everything. The main plus is its location, on the Rue des Moulins, ideal for rounding off a night in the centre of town.

the garage

map - town b3
t 0450 53 64 69
open 10pm-4am
entrance free

If you're wondering where the gaggle of Swedes went when they left the South Bar, they're probably at the Garage - the logical progression from any bar in Cham Sud, and the most reliably busy club in town. The owners cleverly employ beautiful Swedish girls to sell their alcohol, so the large bar is always very busy and very male - and people are generally too busy watching their drinks being made to notice the bill when they arrive. Music is nothing out of the ordinary, though the mirrored dancefloor makes for some entertaining moments watching people watching themselves... the Garage holds regular theme nights - some of which are in questionable taste - and the baguettes on sale in the cloakroom are the only food available in Chamonix at 4am.

the plaza

map - town c4
t 0450 53 63 52
open 10pm-4am
entrance cheap

Next to Safari, and the logical progression from the Pub. A surprisingly small bar but a nice enough place, the main attraction of which is the weekly Scandanavian Party - which as the name suggests is intended to bring in lots of English men hoping to meet Swedish girls. Perhaps surprisingly, Scandinavians go too, and the atmosphere tends to be very lively. Music is generally dancey, with the obligatory style changes through hip-hop, cheese and trance.

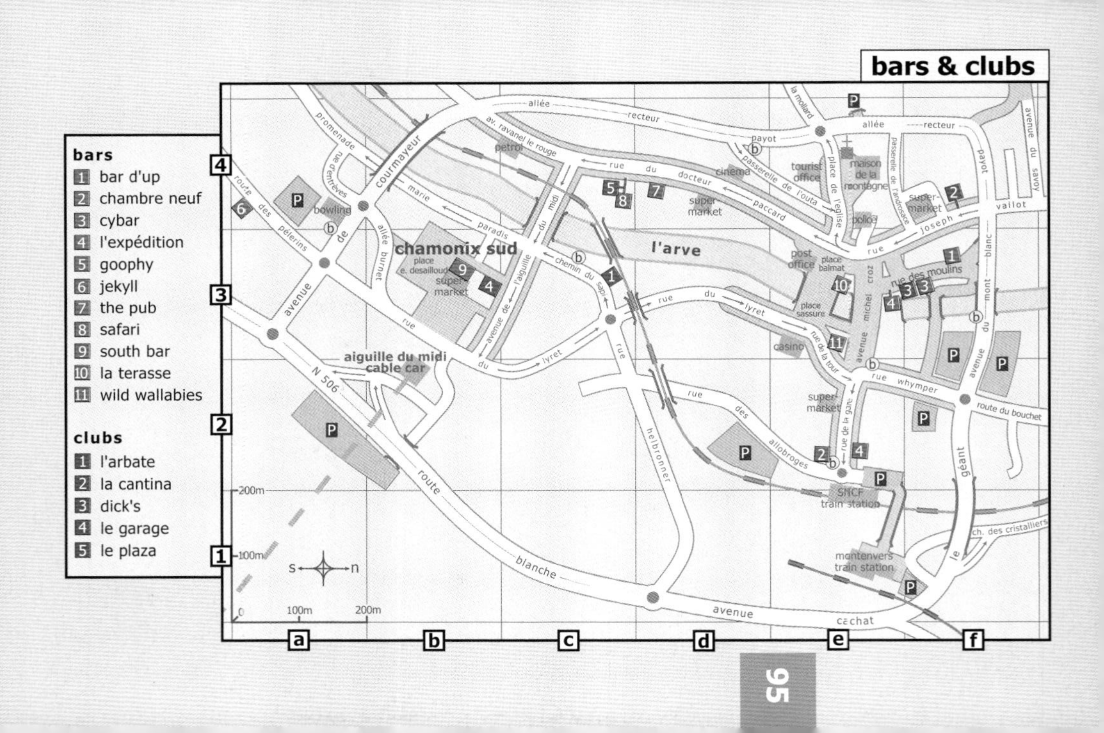
bars & clubs
bars
1 bar d'up
2 chambre neuf
3 cybar
4 l'expédition
5 goophy
6 jekyll
7 the pub
8 safari
9 south bar
10 la terasse
11 wild wallabies
clubs
1 l'arbate
2 la cantina
3 dick's
4 le garage
5 le plaza
chamonix sud
l'arve
aiguille du midi cable car
SNCF train station
montenvers train station
tourist office
maison de la montagne
post office
place balmat
place sassure
place e. desailloud
casino
cinema
police
petrol
bowling
super-market
allée recteur
allée recteur payot
avenue du savoy
vallot
payot
joseph
rue du docteur paccard
passerelle de l'outa
place de l'eglise
passerelle de l'androsace
la mollard
rue des moulins
avenue du mont blanc
avenue michel croz
rue whymper
route du bouchet
rue de la tour
rue de la gare
rue des allobroges
rue du lyret
rue helbronner
chemin du sapi
avenue de l'aiguille du midi
av. ravanel le rouge
promenade marie paradis
courmayeur
rue d'entrèves
allée burnet
avenue de
route des pèlerins
N 506
route blanche
avenue cachat
le géant
ch. des cristalliers
0
100m
200m
s
n
a
b
c
d
e
f
1
2
3
4

hotels

Chamonix's hotel accommodation ranges from exquisite luxury to down-and-dirty dormitories. Per night you can pay over €800 or as little as €12. The hotels below are included for their overall quality in one of four price brackets. Argentière hotels are covered in **argentière**.

snapshot

for...
- cheap as chips - touring
- families - hermitage paccard
- good food - eden
- liveliness - gustavia
- location, location - alpina
- peace & quiet - bois prin
- luxury - albert première

useful information

access - because of how spread out the skiing is, no hotel can be ideally placed for everything - comments are made about each hotel's proximity to lifts and to bus stops. If you are planning to take a car, be aware that many hotels around the centre of town have little or no parking space.

bookings - some hotels will only accept week-long reservations, especially if you are booking a long time in advance. Outside of low season, last-minute bookings are likely to be relatively difficult to make, but the number of beds in the valley means you are likely to find something somewhere - if you are determined enough to spend a day by the phone.

equipment rental - many hotels have a deal with a specific rental shop - they will advise you of this when you check in. Since for the majority of the hotels there are a number of rental shops within easy walking distance, the Chamonix guide does not include a 'nearest rental' entry.

language - every front-of-house employee will speak English, so unless you have a quibble with a cleaning lady you will be able to survive with no French at all. But hotels are where you will notice a difference if you can speak in French. Staff are more likely to be more sympathetic to questions (or complaints) if you make the effort to communicate with them in their language.

prices

The price ranges are approximate figues for a double room per night in high season, including tax but not service.

luxury over €150
mid-range €80-150
budget €30-80
shoestring under €30
All hotels accept most credit cards.

The Shoestring bracket is unique to the Chamonix guide, and is intended for those working with a next-to-negative bank balance.

eden**

map - valley c3
t 0450 53 18 43
(chalet 0450 53 06 57)
f 0450 53 51 50
e relax@hoteledenchamonix.com
i www.hoteleden-chamonix.com
rooms 13
board B&B/½
shuttle ×

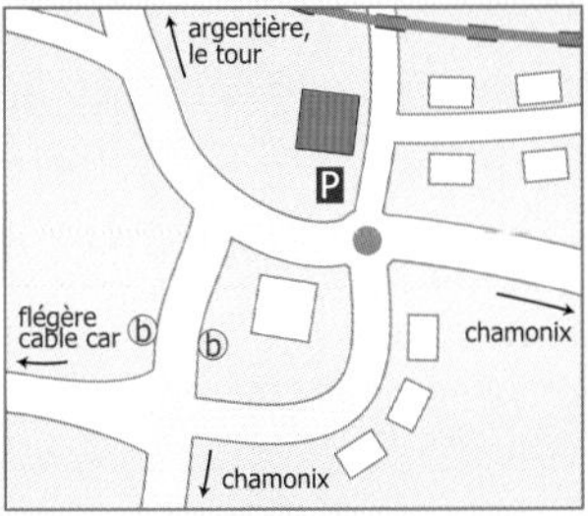

In the small town of Les Praz, the Eden is one of the best-kept secrets in the valley. It is a 1 minute walk to the Les Praz bus stop, and a 2 minute walk to the Flégère base station and the Ravanel & co rental shop. With the liaison cable car that links the Flégère to the Brévent, being 5 minutes drive from the Chamonix town centre is only limiting if you are concerned about your après schedule - Les Praz is not a lively place. But for anyone who wants to avoid the rough and tumble of the bars and clubs (or anyone with their own transport/money for a taxi), staying at the English-run Eden guarantees you a homely welcome that you would be hard pushed to match anywhere else.

Though its lack of luxuries mean that by the French system it only qualifies as a 2* hotel, the rooms are more than comfortable enough to ease away any aches you may have picked up during the day (or night). The restaurant (see **restaurants**) is the best in the valley, the bar doesn't close until the last person leaves... if you are looking for good value, simple comfort, outstanding food, and impeccable and friendly personal service, the Eden is the place to be.

« luxury »

albert première****

map - town f2
t 0450 53 05 09
f 0450 55 95 48
e infos@hammeaualbert.fr
i hammeaualbert.fr
rooms 42
board B&B/½/full
shuttle ✓

The French hotel rating system only goes to 4* - the Albert Première is a strong argument for a 5th. It offers every conceivable luxury, including a Michelin starred restaurant (difficult to get into unless you're a hotel guest), a swimming pool with indoor and outdoor sections, a horse-drawn cart to carry you through the snow to the town, twelve palatial hammeau 'rooms' with - amongst other things - their own fireplaces... it oozes formality, and is very expensive, but it is the summit of professionalism and if you can afford it you should consider nowhere else.

auberge du bois prin****

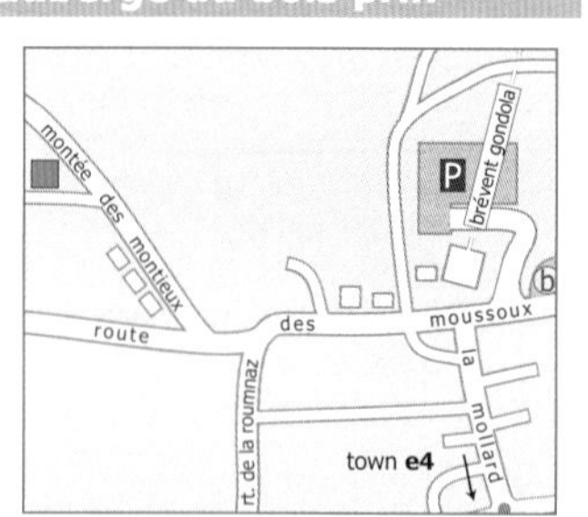

map - valley c2
t 0450 53 33 51
f 0450 53 48 75
e boisprin@relaischateaux.fr
i boisprin.com
rooms 1
board B&B/½/full
shuttle ×

Run by the same family as the Albert Première, the Bois Prin is another Relais & Chateaux. It has the same excellent service and provision of every luxury, but it is out of town in a quiet and spacious location. It is high enough that technically you could ski back to the door - but only if you can find your own way, as there's no piste. It is another splendid example of French attention to detail - and its smaller scale makes it feel more personal. A fine restaurant and bar mean this is a place you may find it difficult to leave after a day's skiing. The nearest rental shop is by the Brévent lift station.

mont blanc ****

map - town e4
t 0450 53 05 64
f 0450 55 89 44
e mont-blanc@chamonixhotels.com
i chamonixhotels.com
rooms 39
board B&B/½/full
shuttle ✓

A beautiful, spacious and excellently located hotel - at the foot of the hill that leads to the Brévent, next to the tourist office and across the road from the Maison de la Montagne. It has a large reception and lounge area, a very formal feeling bar which regularly hosts live musicians, the highly regarded Matalan restaurant, intelligently professional service... and while it doesn't quite have the prestige of the Albert Premiere, it wants for very little and is more convenient for the centre of town.

hermitage-paccard ***

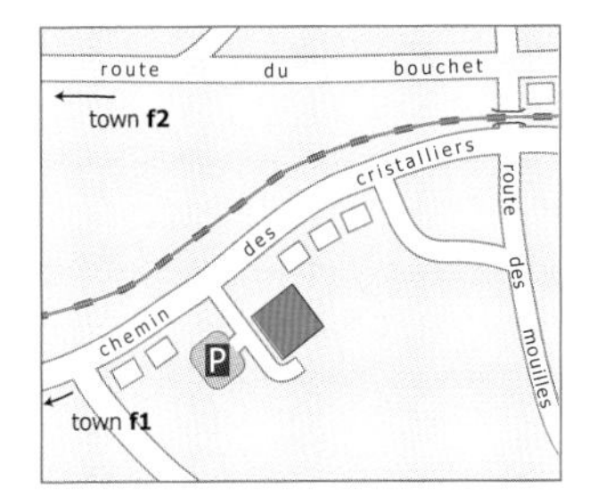

map - valley c2
t 0450 53 13 87
f 0450 55 98 14
e info@hermitage-paccard.com
i hotelhermitagechamonix.com
rooms 30
board B&B/½/full
shuttle ×

A large chalet-style hotel just outside the centre. It has its own grounds, and therefore more space than some of the hotels in town, including an outdoor play area for children. There are both modern and traditionally styled rooms, and facilities include the excellent Cremèrie du Paccard restaurant (see **restaurants**), a gym, a sauna and a games room. It's a 5 minute walk to the town centre - and in the other direction a 5 minute walk to the MBC (see **bars**). All in all it is airy and spacious, friendly and welcoming, and somewhat quieter than the hotels in town - also somewhat more expensive than most 3* hotels, but it is well worth the extra money.

« mid-range »

les aiglons***

map - town a3
t 0450 55 90 93
f 0450 53 51 08
e info@aiglons.com
i aiglons.com
rooms 56
board B&B/½/full
shuttle ×

A large block of a hotel right next to the Cham Sud main bus stop. The Aiglons is far nicer inside than out, the rooms are large and very comfortable, and it has the gym, sauna, and restaurant you would expect from a large hotel. It's a fair walk to the town centre but if you want the Jekyll and l'Impossible (see **bars** and **restaurants** respectively), the Bowling pub, easy access to Cham Sud and to the Chamonix bus, there's nowhere better. Staying in the Aiglons is definitely a choice about where in town you want to be.

alpina***

map - town f3
t 0450 53 47 77
f 0450 55 98 99
e alpina@chamonixhotels.com
i chamonixhotels.com
rooms 136
board B&B/½/full
shuttle ×

If what's important is where you are rather than who you're with, the Alpina is your place. It is very, very large, across the road from the Rue des Moulins and just off the main bus route through town - so you will never have to walk far to get anywhere. You are unlikely to find personal service, but the Alpina has facilities that some smaller hotels in the same price range don't have - a games room, children's entertainment, and a gym, jacuzzi and sauna. The glass-walled Restaurant 4810 on top of the hotel isn't bad, though it is not as good as its view.

gustavia***

map - town e2
t 0450 53 00 31
f 0450 55 86 39
e hotel@hotel-gustavia.com
i hotel-gustavia.com
rooms 47
board B&B/½/full
shuttle ×

The perfect location if you want busy après-ski with your holiday - the Gustavia boasts Chambre Neuf (see **bars**) as one of its rooms and has Goophy's (see **bars**) just across the road. The Chamonix bus stops on the doorstep, and the SNCF train station is across the road - this is not the place for refined luxury, but if you want comfort coupled with absolute convenience, it is on offer here. The clientele is largely English and Scandinavian, and is mostly (but not exclusively) on the young side. The Gustavia also has a resident masseur, a piano room, a terrace (part of Chambre Neuf), very friendly service, and all of Chamonix just outside the front door.

l'oustalet***

map - town c3
t 0450 55 54 99
f 0450 55 54 98
e infos@hotel-oustalet.com
i hotel-oustalet.com
rooms 15
board B&B
shuttle ×

A beautiful mid-size chalet hotel in an excellent location. Situated on the edge of Cham Sud, 2 minutes walk from the Aiguille du Midi cable car and the same from the centre of town - but not on a main route to either, and so never noisy. The Oustalet only offers bed and breakfast accommodation, but its proximity to everything means that dining out is never a hassle, and there is a bar in the hotel for pre-dinner drinks. It is very comfortable throughout, and many rooms have balconies facing Mont Blanc.

savoyarde ***

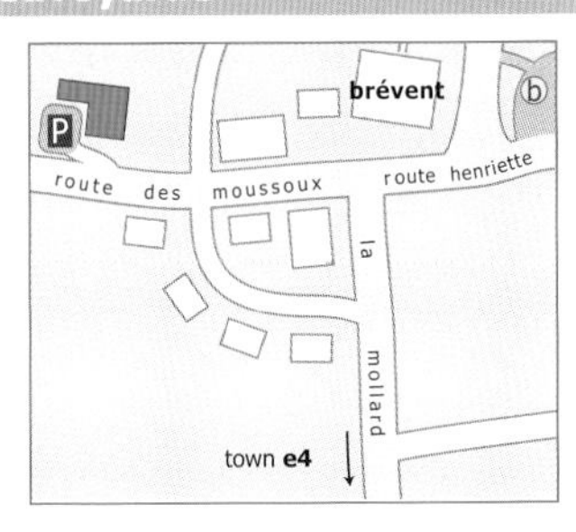

map - valley c2
t 0450 53 00 77
f 0450 55 86 82
e lasavoyarde@wanadoo.fr
i lasavoyarde.com
rooms 14
board B&B/½/full
shuttle ×

A small and cosy hotel in the perfect place to ski the Brévent - at ski boot mph it is literally a 1 minute walk from the gondola station. The Savoyarde is run by the Carrier family (of Bois Prin and Albert Première fame), and has the same attention to detail in a slightly less expensive and less formal environment. Compared to larger hotels what it lacks in luxury it gains in personal service - the only drawback is that the restaurant won't keep you interested for more than a couple of nights and while getting down the hill to town isn't difficult, getting back up to bed might well be. The Savoyarde's nearest rental shop is across the road from the Brévent lift station.

« budget »

richemond**

map - town d4
t 0450 53 08 85
f 0450 55 91 69
e richemond@wanadoo.fr
i richemond.fr
rooms 53
board B&B/½
shuttle ×

The Richemond is the perfect place for those who don't want to pay for luxury but don't want to sacrifice comfort and service. The town centre is just outside the front door, with The Pub (see **bars**) only yards away. The rooms are surprisingly spacious and the 2* rating is due only to the few facilities. The Richemond provides a comfortable bed that's easy to get to.

touring**

map - town e3/4
t 0450 53 59 18
f 0450 53 97 71
e info@hoteltouring-chamonix.com
i hoteltouring-chamonix.com
rooms 24
board B&B
shuttle ×

If you can find the pokey entrance and don't mind the shoebox corridors, the Touring will give you a cheap bed in the middle of town. It is English-run, and so hassle-free, though if you are driving, be aware that you won't be able to park anywhere near the hotel.

« shoestring »

Thanks to the high seasonnaire population and the thriving summer season, there is plenty of low cost accommodation dotted around the valley. Below are two good quality options for particularly meagre budgets.

102 la boule de neige*

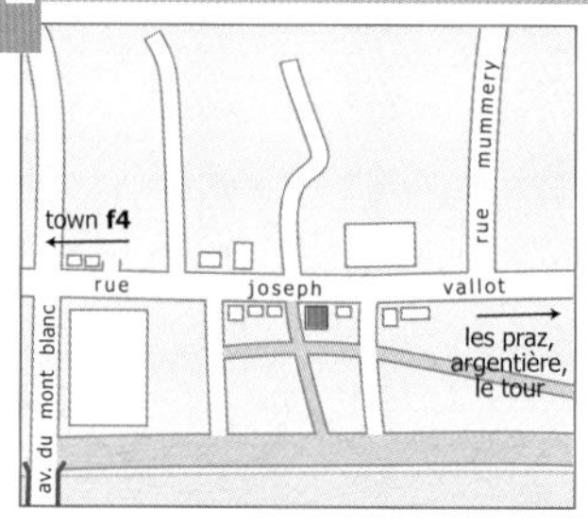

map - valley c2
t 0450 53 04 48
f 0450 55 91 09
e postmaster@hotel-labouledeneige.fr
i hotel-labouledeneige.fr
rooms 9
board B&B
shuttle ×

The Snowball is a little way out of the town centre, but is close to two rental shops and is only a short walk from the Alpina bus stop. The pleasing wooden décor gives it a homely feel, and the bar and restaurant aim their service at the hotel customers - cheap and cheerful.

vagabond (-)

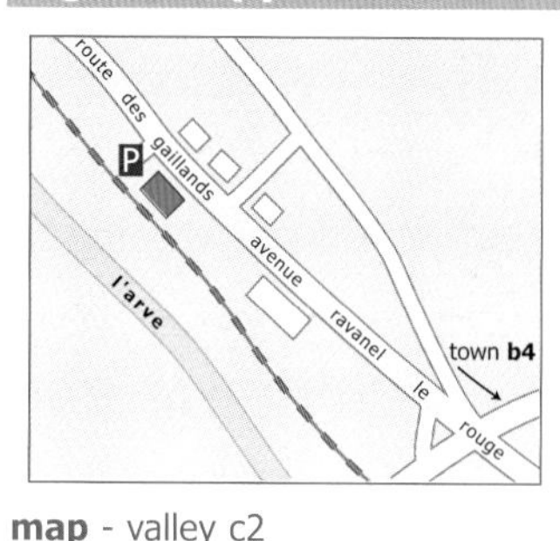

map - valley c2
t 0450 53 15 43
f 0450 53 68 21
e gitevagabond@hotmail.com
i gitevagabond.com
rooms 38 (but see below)
board B&B/½
shuttle ×

The Vagabond is true slumming - it sleeps 38 but there are certainly not 38 rooms. If you make friends easily and don't mind sharing your living and sleeping space with people you've never met before, the Vagabond allows you to stay a night in Chamonix for the price of a pitcher of beer. It is English-run, and has a dark, cramped and excellent bar where you can get to know your next bunk neighbours.

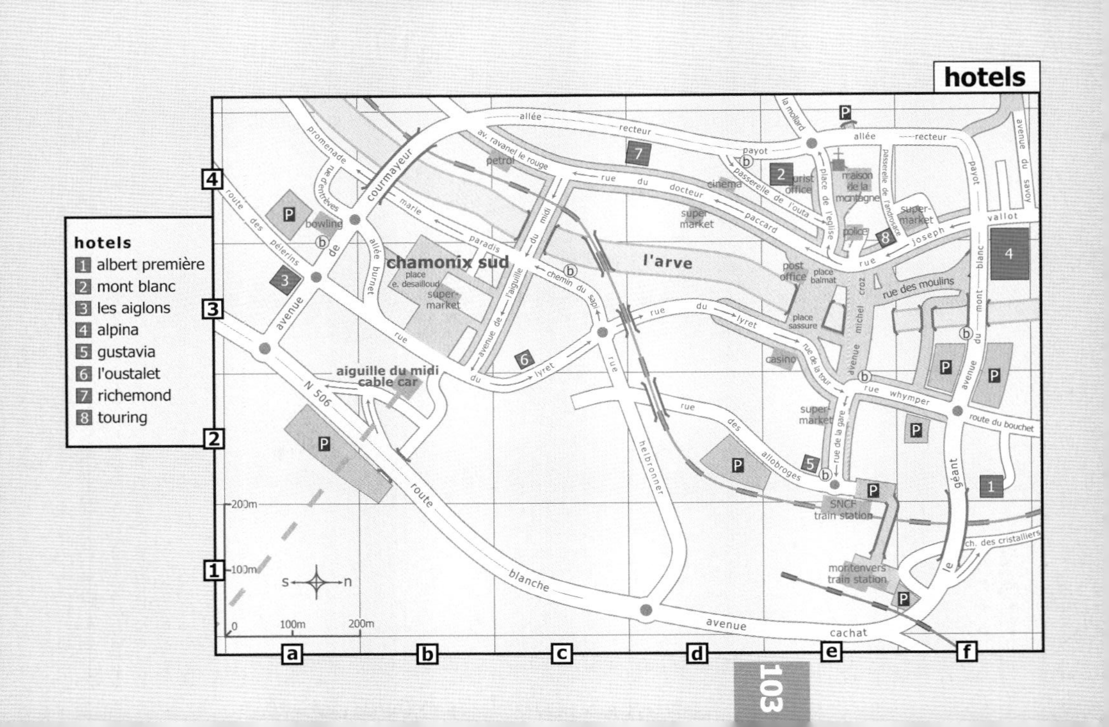
hotels
hotels
1 albert première
2 mont blanc
3 les aiglons
4 alpina
5 gustavia
6 l'oustalet
7 richemond
8 touring
chamonix sud
l'arve
aiguille du midi cable car
post office
place balmat
place sassure
place e. desailloud
super-market
cinema
casino
bowling
petrol
police
maison de la montagne
SNCF train station
montenvers train station
allée recteur payot
av. ravanel le rouge
rue du docteur paccard
passerelle de l'outa
place de l'eglise
passerelle de l'androsace
rue joseph vallot
avenue du savoy
avenue du mont blanc
rue des moulins
avenue michel croz
rue du lyret
rue de la tour
rue whymper
route du bouchet
rue de la gare
rue des allobroges
rue helbronner
avenue cachat le géant
ch. des cristalliers
route blanche
N 506
avenue de l'aiguille du midi
chemin du sapi
rue du lyret
rue de paradis
allée burnet
avenue de courmayeur
promenade marie paradis
rue d'entrèves
route des pèlerins
la mollard
s
n
0
100m
200m
a
b
c
d
e
f
1
2
3
4

argentière

In the shadow of the Grands Montets, the small town of Argentière could be considered a resort in its own right. While Chamonix is attractive for its diversity and cosmopolitan feel, Argentière is the place for people whose priority is a certain kind of skiing. If fifty restaurants, thirty bars and a constant throng of people sounds less attractive to you than being able to walk to the base of the Lognan cable car, it may be worth choosing accommodation a little further up the valley.

getting started

the town

Argentière is 7km away from Chamonix, and just 2km from Le Tour. It is much smaller than Chamonix, consisting basically of just one main street. The map over the page covers the area indicated on the Chamonix valley map (page 17).

getting around

There are bus stops at either end of the main street through the town. When there is no traffic, Chamonix is little more than 10 minutes away, and Le Tour only 2 or 3 minutes.

lift passes

The options for lift passes are the same as for Chamonix - the ChamSki pass is available from the Argentière tourist office and from the cable car station. The Argentière day pass is the most expensive of the valley's four areas, but even so it remains cheaper to buy from day to day if you are only staying a short time. See **getting started**.

equipment rental

The town has a good range of rental shops - some small independent stores on the main street and two larger stores just south of the town centre, including a branch of the Twinner chain (see **skis, boots & boards**). For less conventional equipment, Mont Blanc Sports in the gallerie commerciale has the best overall range.

ski school & guides

Argentière has the same options as Chamonix for lessons and for guiding. The ESF has an Argentière branch, with offices in town and in the Grands Montets cable car building. The guiding company ChamEx is based in Argentière, as is Evolution 2's Panda Club.

the resort

Argentière does not have the volume or range of choice that Chamonix offers. There is little top end accommodation, a limited selection of restaurants, and unless you're on a very short break you won't be able to drink in a different bar every night... but you're unlikely to get bored, and if you do, Chamonix is only a short drive away. All grid references below are to the map on page 107, which shows the layout of Argentière and the Grands Montets cable car station.

restaurants

Argentière has a few mainstream Savoyarde restaurants, all of which serve pleasant food in pleasant surroundings. **la flambée** (**e3**, **t** 0450 54 12 96) is a cheerful and welcoming place, and is good for families and large groups. The restaurant at the hotel **dahu** (**f3**, **t** 0450 54 01 55) serves reliably good food. For something a little smaller, **le carnotzet** (**f3**, **t** 0450 541943) serves fondue and excellent *croûtes* in rather more intimate surrondings.

Of the other restaurants, arguably the best is **harricana** (**d/e3**, **t** 0450 54 22 02) a cosy and bustling place which advertises itself as having an 'innovative' menu. Though the adventurous mix of styles will likely inspire as much intrigue as desire, the food is all very good. For something a little more familiar, **rusticana** (**e3**, **t** 0450 54 00 30) is an English run restaurant-cum-bar with a menu of pseudo-continental dishes, including the somewhat tongue-in-cheek "Toulouse sausages and roast garlic mashed potato". For a change of pace in slightly curious surroundings, **chez anaïs** (**b3**, **t** 0450 54 07 37) doesn't look at all like a restaurant from the outside, but serves good food including some interesting specialities. Next to Harricana, **luigi's** (**e3**, **t** 0450 54 06 60) is a reasonable but unremarkable Italian.

cafés

There isn't really a café in town - the only proper coffee shop is hidden away in the back of the **alp centre** (**e3**). The **hotel dahu** (**f3**) has a terrace if you want to snack in the sunshine, and the **office** (**e2/3**, see **bars**) serves hot drinks and snacks.

bars

The choice of drinking holes is surprisingly limited, and though **rusticana** (**e3**) doubles as a bar, to all extents and purposes you have just two options. The **stone bar** (**f3**) is a good sized and busy place with a pool table and an all-night happy hour arrangement, but the main hub of the après scene is the **office bar** (**e2/3**). As the name suggests, there is nothing very French about the **office**, indeed from décor to service to clientele it is about as un-French a place as you could hope to find. They serve full English breakfast in the morning, Sunday roast on Sundays, and every day from mid-afternoon until early morning it is the home to the various incarnations of Argentière's après revelry.

clubs

There is only one club in Argentière, at the end of the Galerie Commerciale. **space** (**d2**) does not offer anything out of the ordinary, but it does provide the only post-2am entertainment within walking range of the Grands Montets.

accommodation

Though location is a factor in Argentière, it's a small enough place that wherever you choose to stay you're always close enough to the Grands Montets lifts and to a bus stop. There are chalets, apartments and hotels to suit most budgets - though if you are looking to blow your lottery winnings you are better off staying in Chamonix.

hotels

grands montets***

t 0450 53 04 48
i hotel-labouledeneige.fr
rooms 9
board B&B

The easiest way to catch the first lift, and the most luxurious of Argentière's hotels. The chalet-style building is just a couple of minutes walk from the cable car, and the centre of Argentière is about 5 minutes away. All rooms have homely wooden décor, and there is a beautiful indoor pool and an excellent restaurant.

montana***

t 0450 53 04 48
i hotel-labouledeneige.fr
rooms 9
board B&B

In a quiet spot back from the main road, the Montana is just 200m from the Lognan cable car and equally close to the centre of town. It is a chalet-style building with spacious rooms and a pleasant restaurant, good facilities and private parking.

dahu**

t 0450 53 04 48
i hotel-labouledeneige.fr
rooms 9
board B&B

A pleasant and very well situated hotel, right in the centre of town and less than 10 minutes walk from the cable car. The hotel is comfortable and inexpensive, but perhaps the best thing about the Dahu is its restaurant, which serves very good food and which has a terrace (open to guests and public alike) that makes an excellent spot for coffee drinking and mountain watching.

randonneurs*

t 0450 53 04 48
i hotel-labouledeneige.fr
rooms 9
board B&B

A very simple hotel providing beds for cheap. Rooms range from a dormitory to single or double rooms either with basin or shower (but no toilets). It's about as far away from anything as it could be and still be in Argentière, but if you want low-cost digs then this is they.

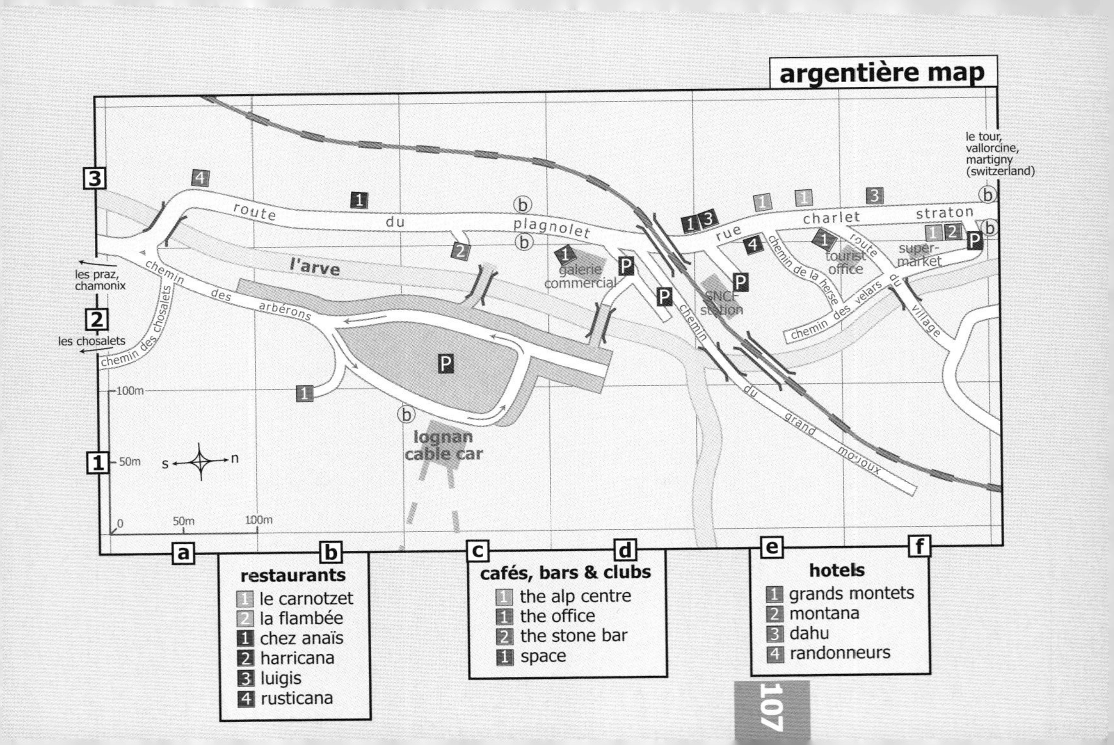
argentière map
route du plagnolet
rue charlet straton
l'arve
chemin des arbérons
chemin des chosalets
chemin de la herse
chemin des velars
route du village
chemin du grand moroux
galerie commercial
tourist office
super-market
SNCF station
lognan cable car
le tour, vallorcine, martigny (switzerland)
les praz, chamonix
les chosalets
0
50m
100m
s
n
restaurants
1 le carnotzet
2 la flambée
1 chez anaïs
2 harricana
3 luigis
4 rusticana
cafés, bars & clubs
1 the alp centre
1 the office
2 the stone bar
1 space
hotels
1 grands montets
2 montana
3 dahu
4 randonneurs

activities

When the lifts are closed because of too little or - more frustratingly - too much snow, there a few things to keep you occupied. See the **directory** for all contact details.

sport

sports centre & swimming - the *centre sportif*, just past the ice rink, has a wide range of facilities - a large indoor swimming complex, a small but excellent weights room, a solarium, sauna, hammam, a small bouldering wall, tennis and squash courts.

The *centre nautique* (swimming pool) is open every day 2pm-8pm, and on Friday evenings until 9pm. One of the indoor pools is 25m long and there is also a jacuzzi, a water slide, and swimming lessons are available. The only problem is the dress code - men are only allowed to swim in speedos.

For either the *centre sportif* or *nautique* you can pay by the visit, though for anyone with long term plans it is cheaper to buy passes, which are available for twelve visits or on a monthly basis.

bowling - the Bowling Pub in Cham Sud has eight lanes, a range of pool and snooker tables, and a bar. It is open every day 5pm-2am (or from 2pm on bad weather days).

helicoptor tours - Chamonix Mont-Blanc helicoptors and SAF Chamonix helicoptors run daily panoramic flights around the valley.

ice climbing - Chamonix has ice climbing for all levels of ability. It is a good place to start the sport - not least because there are so many willing guides around - but there is also a huge range of challenging ice and mixed routes for the more experienced. Contact any of the guiding companies, though ChamEx are particularly recommended.

ice hockey - more of a spectator's sport, the indoor ice rink (north of town off the Route du Bouchet, **town f2**), hosts Chamonix's own hockey team, and on occasion the French national team. Games take place on Saturday evenings, and are advertised on banners, posters and fliers.

ice skating - the covered and outdoor ice rinks are next to the *centre sportif*. The covered rink is open every day 10am-12pm and 3pm-6pm except Wednesday afternoons and 9pm-11pm on Wednesday evenings. The outdoor ice rink is open every day depending on the weather.

parapenting - Chamonix is the ideal place for paragliding. The most common launch point for tandem jumps is on the Brévent, alongside the Altitude 2000 chair, though it is also possible to jump from the Aiguille du Midi. The main landing spot is the Savoy beginners' slope, right in the middle of town. The ESF, the Companie des Guides, Evo 2, Ski Sensations and a specialist company called Summlts (next to Invasion Snowboards, **town f4**) all offer tandem jumps.

salle de jeux - almost a sport, the arcade at the end of the Rue des Moulins (**town e3**) has a number of more-or-less up to date video games, should you be short on adrenaline and high on expendable cash.

tennis - the tennis club has 2 covered courts and 1 squash court, and is open every day 9am-12:15am and 3pm-7:15pm. You can hire rackets if you forgot to pack yours.

culture

casino - prominently placed across the road from the Place Sassure (**town e3**), the casino is perhaps best used as a landmark for navigating your way around town, but if you have the gambling urge it is open every day from midday until the small hours. Along with the various other means of losing your money, you can spend it in the bar and in the casino's own restaurant.

cinema - on the Rue Paccard (**town d4**) the Chamonix cinema has three screens, and usually has one film in English every day - look out for 'VO' (*version originale*) on the schedule. Films run afternoon and evening in much the same way as in Enlgand, though there's not much in the way of popcorn or pic n' mix, so if you want to munch you should buy food beforehand. An extra screening is shown on bad weather days.

guided tour - there is a two hour guided walking tour of the town on one morning every week. Contact the tourist office for more details.

dr jivago - if you want a horse-drawn tour of the local area, Dr Jivago is your man. He's not very talkative, but travelling through the snow in a carriage is quite enough on its own. It's not cheap, but up to six can go at a time. He and his horse are based at the west end of the Avenue Michel Croz (**town e3**).

museum - the Musée Alpin, just off the Avenue Michel Croz (**town e3**), is not so much a museum of Chamonix as of the surrounding mountains. It has displays featuring early maps of the area, a history of the attempts to climb Mont Blanc, the story of the development of various winter sports including the first Winter Olympics in 1924, a history of the tourism in the area, a crystal collection, and also often has a specialist exhibition which will be advertised around town. It is open 2pm-7pm and 11am-7pm during school holidays.

children

The Chamonix valley is well equipped with facilities for children. A few of the tour operators offer day-time childcare and kids clubs, and both the ESF and Evolution 2 offer instruction aimed specifically at young learners.

a word of caution

Children can find it difficult to adapt to the thinner air at high altitude, particularly when coupled with the excitement of places like the Aiguille du Midi, where just the cable car is likely to get their pulse going.

tour operators

Many operators have discounted or free child places in their chalets and some also include free ski and boot hire, lift passes or ski lessons for childen. In addition, a few operators run childcare programmes. The forerunner is probably **esprit** - children are a key part of their business - and in Chamonix and Argentière their programme includes everything from a nursery (for children as young as 4 months) to after-ski school care (for children aged between 3 and 11). **crystal** has a dedicated crêche and nanny service for all children staying in their accommodation, and free evening babysitting in one chalet (Chalet Bernadette). **club med**, as you would expect from a leading families operator, has a full day programme for children aged between 4 and 10.

childcare

babysitters - the tourist office will point you in the direction of qualified nannies and babysitters - though Chamonix is crawling with seasonnaires in need of Euros, so if you would prefer English-speaking childcare at negotiable rates you won't have to look far. Just ask behind the bar in somewhere like the Cybar or Goophy's.

kindergarten/crêche - the **halte de garderie** (**t** 0450 53 36 68) on Promenade du Fori will look after children aged between 3 months and 3 years, while the **maison pour tous** (**t** 0450 53 12 24) next to the halte de garderie organises leisure programmes for children aged between 4 and 11 years.

lift passes

The ChamSki pass has a number of options aimed at families and children. Under 16s ('Juniors') and Under 12s ('Kids') get a basic reduction in the price of the pass, and there are also deals on 6-day passes for adult and child combinations. For under 12s who have never skied before, there is a cheaper version of the ChamStart pass, which gives access to the valley-floor lifts. See **getting started**.

ski school

The ESF (see **ski schools** in **getting started**) has 30 specialist children's instructors, and runs lessons for children over the age of 3. Private lessons are the same as for adults, and group lessons in the Kid's Club run at the Savoy slope in Chamonix or in the Jardin d'Enfants in Argentière. Lessons run from Monday to Saturday, and length varies by the time of the season: from December to the beginning of February they are either 2 or 4 hours long, changing to 2½ or 5 hours from February to the end of the season. There are various different packages on offer, including provision of lunch, child care, and a full 6 day program.

Children must wear a helmet to join a group lesson. All the ski rental shops have helmets for hire - though make sure you get one that fits well. Many a tantrum has been thrown because of an ill-fitting helmet.

other options

panda club

t 0450 54 04 76
open Sundays to Fridays
age 2½ - 12 years

Evolution 2's children's branch, based in Argentière, runs a schedule of skiing lessons for anyone over the age of 2½, which basically means any child who is a confident walker. Options include 2 hour and 4 hour lessons, half days (morning or afternoon) and full days, and over Easter the ski lessons combine with a mulit-activities programme.

activities

There are events for children throughout the season, ranging from the arrival of Santa Claus in the lead-up to Christmas, to childrens competitions during the ChamJam - as well as the more regular activities listed below.

on the snow - the ESF organise a torch-lit descent during February and March on the Grands Montets.

off the snow - children under 6 years old can use the swimming pool at the Centre Sportif for free. The water garden there is open on Saturdays 10am-11am for children aged between 6 months and 4 years. They can also use the bouldering wall, although children under 10 must be accompanied by a guide, and children aged between 10 and 14 must be accompanied by an adult.

eating & drinking

Most of Chamonix's restaurants and cafés welcome children, and some offer a childrens menu. **munchie**, **gecko**, and **le pitz** (see **restaurants**) are particularly good, as are the restaurants in **wild wallabies** and **goophy** (see **bars**). Children are also generally allowed into the bars and pubs, and it is up to you whether they drink - nobody is likely to bat an eyelid if a child or teenager drinks wine or has a beer with their parents.

the a-z

directory

listings
All 0450 or 06 numbers need the French international prefix (0033) if dialled from the UK.

Where applicable, references are given to the town map.

accidents
If you have an accident on the slopes, you will be taken to the nearest doctor unless you specify a particular one. To confirm you can pay for treatment you will need a credit card and your insurance details. At some point, contact your insurance company to check whether they want to arrange your transport home - and ask your doctor for a medical certificate confirming you are fit to travel.

If you see an accident on the slopes, tell the nearest rescue centre, usually found at the top or bottom of lifts.

activities
bowling 196 Avenue de Courmayer, Chamonix Sud **t** 0450 53 74 37

cinema programme listings **t** 0450 53 03 39, bookings **t** 0450 55 89 98

dog sleighs
huskydalen t 0450 47 77 24/0684 99 34 67
also see **evolution 2** under **guides**.

ice climbing see **guides**.

ice skating t 0450 53 12 36

parapenting
les ailes du mont blanc t 0620 46 55 57/0450 53 96 72,
i lesailesdumontblanc.free.fr
haut vol t 0450 53 98 01/0680 03 24 74,
summits parapente t 0450 53 50 14, **i** summits.fr

sports centres & swimming
centre sportif richard bozon
t 0450 53 09 07, **i** sports.chamonix.com

tennis
t 0450 53 38 40, **open** 9am-12:15pm 5pm-7:15pm.

snow activities
cross-country skiing
chamonix t 0450 53 11 15
argentière t 0450 54 14 22

heliskiing
chamonix mont-blanc hélicoptères t 0450 54 13 82
also see any of the guiding companies, under **guides**.

night-skiing at Les Houches - see **other resorts**.

snowshoeing organised with a guide, see under **guides**.

aiguille du midi
automated reservations line 0892 68 00 67

directory

apartments & private chalets

centrale de réservations t 0450 53 23 33, **i** reservation.chamonix.com
chalet cascade t 0773 098 7600
i chaletcascade.com
chamonix house
i chamonixhouse.com
cham lodge t 0207 373 4013
i chamlodge.com
chamonix direct t 0450 55 90 37
i chamonix.direct.com
interhome t 0208 891 1294
i interhome.co.uk

banks & ATMs

banque Laydernier and **banque de Savoie** on Place Balmat open Monday to Friday 9am-12pm and 3pm-6pm. All have 24 hour ATMs, but plan ahead if you want money at weekends as they can run out.

car hire

geneva airport
ALAMO t 0041 22 717 8430
i alamo.com
AVIS t 0041 22 929 0330 **i** avis.com
easycar t 0906 333 3333
i easycar.com
europcar t 0041 22 798 1110
i europcar.com
hertz t 0870 844 8844 **i** hertz.com

chamonix
europcar t 0450 53 63 40, at the BP petrol station (**c4**).

carte d'hôte

If you are staying in a hotel, you should receive one when you arrive. The card gives you reductions for some public facilities including parking and the *centre sportif*.

casino t 0450 53 07 65

church services

The église Saint-Michel (**e4**) holds Catholic services in French at 6:30pm on Saturdays and 10:30am and 6pm on Sundays. A Protestant service is held at 24 Passage du Temple on the 1st and 3rd Sundays in December, January, March and April at 10am and every Sunday at 10am in February.

customs

As France is part of the EU, there are few restrictions on what UK visitors can take out for personal use.

doctor

There are ten medical practices in Chamonix, so you can take your pick. The nearest hospital is in Les Favrands, just beyond Chamonix Sud. Also see **emergencies**.

driving

general - carry a valid driver's licence, proof of ownership, your insurance certificate and an emergency triangle.

speed limits - in built-up areas the speed limit is 50km/h (unless indicated). The limit is 90km/h on all other roads, 110km/h on toll-free motorways and 130km/h on toll motorways. The last stretch of the Route Blanche leading up to Chamonix is a notorious spot for police speed traps, especially at weekends. Foreign drivers are given spot fines.

signs & rules - motorways in France have blue signs. Most operate a péage (toll) system. You must wear a seatbelt in the front and back of a car. Children under 12 must sit in the back and babies and young children must be placed in special baby/young child seats.

dvds and videos

There is a rental shop on the road behind the Brioche'In (**f4**) and one on the Avenue de L'Aiguille du Midi in Chamonix Sud (**c3**).

electricity

220 volts/50hz ac. Appliances use a two-pin plug - adaptors are readily available form electrical stores or supermarkets.

emergency numbers

emergency centre/fire brigade t 18
(from a mobile) t 112
police t 0450 53 75 02
ambulance t 0450 53 46 20
24/7 road assistance t
mountain rescue t 0450 53 16 89
euro emergency t
central hospital t 0450 53 84 00
on-call **dentist t** 0450 66 17 19
doctor t 0450 53 48 48
pharmacy t 0450 53 36 79

guides

chamonix experience t/f 0450 53 73 87/88, **i** chamex.com
compagnie des guides de chamonix mont-blanc t/f 0450 53 00 88/48 04, **i** chamonix-guides.com, open 8:30am-12pm, 3:30pm-7:30pm.
evolution 2 t/f 0450 55 93 03/91 33, **i** evolution2.com
ski sensations t 0450 53 56 46 **i** ski-sensations.com

health

An E111 form (available from any UK post office) entitles you to treatment under the French health system. While you have to pay for your treatment when you receive it, you can then get a refund for up to 70% of medical expenses - as long as you keep all your receipts.

insurance

It is essential to have personal insurance covering wintersports and the cost of any ambulances, helicopter rescue and emergency repatriation - all these services are very expensive. Insurance policies differ greatly - some exclude off-piste skiing or cover it only if you are with a guide, so you need to check the terms and conditions carefully.

internet/email

The main internet centre is the **cybar** (**f3**), which has 24 stations. There is an internet café is in the **galerie blanc neige** (**c4**), where you can buy credit - there is also a 24 hour terminal outside. Lots of bars have one or more stations: **eldorado** (**c4**) has 5, as does **macdonalds** (**e3**). **chambre neuf** (**e2**) and **safari** (**c4**) each have one, and there is one in the **galerie alpina** (**f3**). In Argentière there is a terminal in the **galerie commmerciale** (**d2**) and in the **office** (**e2/3**). All the terminals are inexpensive and prices are similar, with an initial charge and then a per minute addition.

language
English is widely spoken, though an attempt at French is widely appreciated.

laundry & dry cleaning
laverie du mont blanc on the Avenue de l'Aiguille du Midi and **pressing de l'arve** in the Galerie Alpina.

library
open (**t** 0450 53 34 82) 2:30pm-6:30pm from Tuesday to Saturday and 9am-12pm on Wednesdays.

lift pass company
compagnie du mont blanc (**t/f** 0450 53 14 14/ 92 44) - for sales see **lift passes** in **getting started**.

maps
All of the *libraries* sell IGN maps (the French equivalent of the OS).

market
Chamonix is a market town, and on Saturday mornings the car park next to the Alpina hotel (**f2/3**) is taken over by stalls selling local produce.

massage
anne de sampigny, t 0680 96 13 52, **le bachal t** 0450 53 05 09, **institut apparence t** 0450 53 11 45, **institut de beauté mixte apollon & messaline t** 0450 53 42 31, **nikki jennings t** 0638 73 63 51 (home visits).

money
The currency is the Euro (€). €1 is equivalent to 100 centimes. Notes come in anything from €10 to €500. You can exchange money in all the banks in Chamonix during the week, and also at Geneva airport and in major train stations. There is a bureau de change on Rue de la Gare (**e2**) and one on Place Balmat (**e3**) for currency exchange open 7 days a week. In 2003, the average exchange rate for UK£1 = (*approx*) €1.6

newspapers
Some of the *libraries* stock a small selection of English newspapers, or you can read them in the Cybar.

other resorts
courmayeur - is surprisingly close. A trip through the Mont Blanc tunnel only takes 20 minutes - and offers good food and good skiing below the tree-line. A ChamSki pass of 4 or more days allows you one days free skiing in Courmayeur.

directory

les houches - at the foot of the Chamonix valley, Les Houches is home to the Kandahar run used in the World Cup downhill (see **events**). It is separate from the rest of the Chamonix valley and is not covered by the ChamSki pass (though it is on the Mont-Blanc pass). The skiing is not as extensive as in the valley's main areas, but as with Courmayeur it is below the tree-line and is a good place to head in poor visibility.

parking

Parking on the roads is allowed where indicated - in town there are many pay & display spaces along the roads, all of which are free over lunchtime. At weekends the car parks become very busy.

passport photos

There are photo booths in the Tourist Office (**e4**) and at the SNCF Train Station (**e1**).

petrol

Petrol stations are few and far between - there are only three in the whole valley and none north of Chamonix. They do not open late or have 24-hour self service.

pharmacies

pharmacie de l'aiguille du midi (**t** 0450 53 40 93) on Avenue de l'Aiguille du Midi, **pharmacie de la vallee** (**t** 0450 53 13 69) on Rue Joseph Vallot, **pharmacie des alpes** (**t** 0450 53 15 45) on Rue Paccard and **pharmacie du mont blanc** (**t** 0450 53 12 61) on Place d l'Eglise.

police

gendarmerie (**t** 0450 53 00 55) 111 Route de la Mollard
police municipale (**t** 0450 53 75 02) at 48 Rue de L'Hotel-de-Ville.

post

The **post office** (**t** 0450 53 15 90) on the Place Balmat (**e3**) opens Monday to Friday 8:30am-12pm and 2pm-6pm and Saturday 8am-12pm.

public holidays

December	6 - St Nicholas Day
	25 - Christmas Day
	26 - St Stephen's day
January	1 - New Year's Day
March/April	Good Friday, Easter Sunday & Monday

radio stations

local radio stations are as follows:
Fun Radio 94.9FM
Radio Mont Blanc 89.2FM
NRJ 100.4FM
Couleur 3 99.9FM

safety on the mountain

avalanche danger - the risk of avalanche is graded from 1 to 5.
1 & 2. (yellow) low risk.
3 & 4. (checked yellow and black) moderate risk, caution advised when skiing off-piste
5. (black) high risk, off-piste skiing strongly discouraged.
The risk is displayed on a flag at the

main lift stations and on the road through Argentière, but if you are in any doubt about where it is safe to ski, ask the advice of the lift operators.

food & drink - a skiing holiday is not the time to start a diet. Your body expends energy keeping warm and exercising so it's a good idea to eat a decent breakfast, and carry some chocolate or sweets with you.
The body dehydrates more quickly at altitude and whilst exercising. You need to drink a lot (of water) each day to replace the moisture you lose.

rules of conduct - the International Ski Federation publishes conduct rules for all skiers and boarders, summarised below:
1. respect - do not endanger or prejudice others.
2. control - ski in control, adapting speed and manner to ability, the conditions and the traffic.
3. choice of route - the uphill skier must choose his route so he does not endanger skiers ahead.
4. overtaking - allowed above or below, right or left, but leave enough room for the overtaken skier.
5. entering & starting a run - look up and down the piste when doing so.
6. stopping on the piste - avoid stopping in narrow places or where visibility is restricted.
7. climbing - keep to the side of the piste when climbing up or down.
8. signs & markings - respect these.
9. assistance - every skier must assist at accidents.
10. identification - all involved in an accident (including witnesses) must exchange details.

seasonnaires

jobs - most UK ski companies recruit seasonal workers - interviewing normally starts in May, although there may still be vacancies at the start of the season. Jobs become available throughout the season, because of staff turnover, illness or accidents. Either contact the companies directly (see **tour operators**), or go through a ski job recruitment website, such as **natives.co.uk**.

in resort - Chamonix has too many seasonnaires for there to be a closely-knit community. Most season workers are English or Swedish, and groups form mostly through where you live or what your job is. There is an implied friendship which makes the majority of the community very welcoming, though in places it can feel a little cliquey - especially among some bar workers.

prices - Probably half of the bars offer small price reductions for seasonnaires - but as with most resorts the best way to get cheap drinks is to get to know a barman, or to be one yourself.

directory

lift passes - you can only buy season passes from the Montenvers train station (**e1**). They are recorded on a computer, so if you break your pass (which you probably will) they will provide you with a new one. After the third replacement they will start to charge... if you lose your pass, it's lost. They won't give you another one.

work permits - you don't need any kind of permit to work in France.

shopping

Most shops open every day (except public holidays) 8:30am-12:30pm and 2:30pm-7pm.

food

supermarkets - Chamonix has five supermarkets - the **marché U** (**f4**), a **grand casino** (**b3**) and 3 **petit casinos**.

bread - there are any number of boulangeries in town. The best is **le petrin** on the Place du Mont-Blanc (**f2**).

cheese - is best bought from the supermarket, if you can stand the queues. Places like the **refuge payot** and **alpage des aiguilles** sell good quality cheeses but at somewhat inflated prices.

wine - as with cheeses, the best wines are available away from the tourist traps like the **refuge payot**. The **comptoir du caviste** (**f/g4**) has an excellent and well priced selection along with knowledgeable and friendly ownership, and the **caves ribeyrolles** (**f1**) is a huge wine warehouse.

clothes - the larger ski shops stock most outdoor brands, in addition to which there are outlet stores for **helly hansen**, **patagonia**, **quiksilver** and **rip curl**. All are situated on Rue du Docteur Paccard.

ski & board servicing

WWS a specialist servicing shop, is next to cappadoce (**b3**) in Cham Sud.

telephone

Public phones boxes are located throughout the town and accept coins or phonecards, which can be bought from the post office, tabacs, and train and petrol stations. All local and calls within Europe are cheaper 7pm-8am during the week and all day at the weekend. The international dialling code for France is **0033**; the free international operator **12**; the international directory information **1159**; and national directory information **111**. There are three mobile phone networks: Bouyges Telecom, France telecom/Orange and SFR.

time

France is always one hour ahead of England.

tipping

All food bills include a service charge,

though it is common to make an addition for drinks or for noticeably good service.

tour operators

mainstream

airtours t 0870 238 7777 **i** mytravel.com
club med t 0207 348 3333 **i** clubmed.co.uk
crystal t 0870 160 6040 **i** crystalski.co.uk
first choice t 0870 754 3477 **i** fcski.co.uk
inghams t 0208 780 4433 **i** inghams.co.uk
neilson t 0870 333 3356 **i** neilson.com
thomson t 0870 888 0254 **i** thomson-ski.co.uk

specialist

esprit t 01252 618 300 **i** esprit-holidays.co.uk
flexiski t 0870 909 0754 **i** flexiski.com
hand made holidays t 01453 885 599 **i** handmade-holidays.co.uk
lagrange t 0207 371 6111 **i** lagrange-holidays.co.uk
made to measure t 0124 353 3333 **i** madetomeasureholidays.com
rocky mountain t 0870 366 5442 **i** rockymountain.co.uk
ski activity t 01738 840 888 **i** skiactivity.co.uk
ski total t 0870 163 3633 **i** skitotal.com
uptoyou t 0871 220 3099 **i** uptoyou.com

chamonix specific

bigfoot t 0870 300 5874 **i** bigfoot-travel.co.uk
boardnlodge t 0207 916 2275 **i** boardnlodge.com
collineige t 0127 624 262 **i** collineige.com
high mountain holidays t 0199 377 5540 **i** highmountain.co.uk
huski t 0207 938 4844 **i** huski.com
mcnab mountain sports t 01546 830 243 **i** macnab.co.uk
mountain discovery t 0450 447 288 **i** mountaindiscovery.co.uk
mountain & molehills t 0138 675 1338 **i** alpinechalets.co.uk

weekend specialists

4 feet deep t 0207 064 4777 **i** 4feetdeep.com
alpine weekends t 0208 944 9762, **i** alpineweekends.co.uk
momentum ski t 0207 371 9111 **i** momentum.uk.com
finlay ski t 0157 322 6611 **i** finlayski.com
ski weekend t 01367 241 636 **i** skiweekend.com
white roc t 0207 792 1188 **i** whiteroc.co.uk

tourist information

chamonix - the tourist office (**t/f** 0450 53 00 24/58 90, **i** chamonix.com) is opposite the Maison de la Montagne (**e4**) and opens Monday to Sunday 8:30am-12:30pm and 2pm-6pm and on Saturdays and Sundays of the Christmas and February holidays

glossary

a

approach skis - short skis used by boarders as a faster (though more expensive) alternative to snowshoes.
arête - a sharp ridge.
avalanche - a rapid slide of snow down a slope.
avalanche transceiver - device used when skiing off-piste, which can both emit and track a high frequency signal to allow skiers lost in an avalanche or crevasse to be found.

b

binding - attaches boot to ski.
black run/piste - difficult, generally steeper than a red piste.
blood wagon - a stretcher on runners used by ski patrollers to carry injured skiers off the mountain.
blue run/piste - easy, generally wide with a gentle slope.
bubble - see '**gondola**'.
button (or Poma) **lift** - for 1 person. Skis and boards run along the ground, whilst you sit on a small 'button' shaped seat.

c

cable car - a large box-shaped lift, running on a thick cable over pylons high above the ground, which carry up to 250 people per car.
carving - a recently developed turning technique used by skiers and boarders to make big, sweeping turns across the piste.
carving skis - shorter and fatter than traditional skis, used for carving turns.
chair lift - like a small and uncomfortable sofa, which scoops you and your skis off the ground and carries you up the mountain. Once on, a protective bar with a rest for your skis holds you in place. Can carry 2-6 people.
combat skiing - tree-skiing.
couloir - a 'corridor' between two ridges, normally steep and narrow.
crampons - spiked fittings attached to outdoor or ski boots to climb mountains or walk on ice.

d

draglift or (T-bar) - for 2 people. Skis and boards run on the ground, whilst you lean against a small bar.
drop-off - a sharp increase in gradient.

e

edge - the metal ridge on the border of each side of the ski.

f

FIS - Federation Internationale du Ski
flat light - lack of contrast caused by shadow or cloud, making it very difficult to judge depth and distance.
freeriding, **freeskiing** - off-piste skiing.
freestyle - skiing involving jumps.

g

glacier - a slow-moving ice mass formed thousands of years ago and fed each year by fresh snow.
gondola (or bubble) - an enclosed lift, often with seats.
green run/piste - very shallow gradient for beginners.

h

heliskiing - off-piste skiing on routes only accessible by helicopter.
high mountain tour (orange) - not

groomed, maintained or patrolled, and considered more difficult than all pistes and itinerary routes.
high season - weeks when the resort is (generally) at full capacity.

i

itinerary route (yellow) – not groomed, maintained or patrolled. Generally more difficult, at least in part, than a black piste. Can be skied without a guide.

k

kicker - jump.

l

ledgy - off-piste conditions in which there are many short, sharp drop-offs.
low season - beginning and end of the season and the least popular weeks in mid-January.

m

mid season - reasonably popular weeks in which the resort is busy but not full.
mogul - bump, small or large, on or off piste. A large mogulled area is called a mogul field.

o

off-piste - area away from marked, prepared and patrolled pistes.

p

parallel turn - skis turn in parallel.
piste - ski run marked, groomed and patrolled, and graded in terms of difficulty - green, blue, red or black.
piste basher - bulldozer designed to groom pistes by smoothing snow.
pisteur - ski piste patroller.
Poma - see '**button lift**'.
powder - fresh, unbashed or untracked snow.

r

raquettes - see '**snowshoes**'.
red run/piste - intermediate, normally steeper than a blue piste, although a flatish piste may be a red because it is narrow, has a steep drop-off or because snow conditions are worse than on other pistes.

s

schuss - a straight slope down which you can ski very fast.
seasonnaire - individual who lives (and usually works) in a ski resort for the season.
skis - technology has changed in the last 10 years. New skis are now shorter and wider. When renting, you will be given a pair approx. 5-10cms shorter than your height.
ski patrol - team of piste patrollers.
skins - artificial fur attached to ski base, for ski touring.
snow-chains - chains attached to car tyres so that it can be driven (cautiously) over snow or ice.
snowshoes - footwear resembling tennis rackets which attach to shoes, for walking on soft snow.
spring snow - granular, heavy snow conditions common in late season (when daytime temperatures rise causing snow to thaw and re-freeze).
steeps - a slope with a very steep gradient.

t

T-bar - see '**draglift**'.

w

white-out - complete lack of visibility caused by enveloping cloud cover.

index

index

the authors

Isobel Rostron and Michael Kayson are snowsport enthusiasts who met while taking time out from real life to indulge their passion - Isobel to get it out of her system and Michael to engrain it further. Michael's approach having won, they decided that a return to real life was overrated and came up with a cunning plan to make their passion their work. The result was snowmole.

acknowledgements

None of this would have been possible without the help and support of many people:

Andrew Lilley, Emily Rostron & John Morgan, Angela Horne, Jos Cooke-Priest, Julian Horne, Ali & Nick Smith, Henry & Katie Fyson, Ali Sallaway & Steven Houseman, Tom Fyson, Peter & Christine Rostron, Tom Wedgewood, the boys, Russ Cole, Ben Slatter, Rupert Harbour, Jane Rostron & Tamlyn Stone, Chris Sheedy, Ruff, ginger beer and maltesers and everybody at Cambrian Printers.

accuracy and updates

We have tried our best to ensure that all the information included is accurate at the date of publication. However, because places change - improve, get worse, or even close - you may find things different when you get there. Also, everybody's experience is different and you may not agree with our opinion.

If we learn of any major changes after we have published this guide, we will let you know on our website - www.snowmole.com. You can also help us, in two ways: by letting us know of any changes you notice and by telling us what you think - good or bad - about what we've written. If you have any comments, ideas or suggestions, please write to us at: snowmole, 45 Mysore Road, London, SW11 5RY or send an email to comments@snowmole.com

available from 2004

the snowmole guides to...

- **courchevel les 3 vallées**
- **méribel les 3 vallées**
- **tignes les 3 vallées**
- **val d'isère espace killy**
- **val thorens espace killy**